ASTD Training Basics Series

TRAINER Basics

GEORGE M. PISKURICH

A Complete, How-to Guide to Help You:

▶ Understand What a Trainer Does and Why

▶ Develop Key Must-Have Skills for Success

▶ Apply Your Knowledge Today

ASTD
Linking People,
Learning & Performance

ASTD Press is an internationally renowned source of insightful and practical information on workplace learning and performance topics, including training basics, evaluation and return-on-investment (ROI), instructional systems development (ISD), e-learning, leadership, and career development.

Ordering information: Books published by ASTD Press can be purchased by visiting our website at store.astd.org or by calling 800.628.2783 or 703.683.8100.

Library of Congress Control Number: 2003113724

ISBN-10: 1-56286-350-9
ISBN-13: 978-1-56286-350-0

Acquisitions and Development Editor: Mark Morrow
Copyeditor: Karen Eddleman
Interior Design and Production: Kathleen Schaner
Cover Design: Ana Ilieva
Cover Illustration: Phil and Jim Bliss

Printed by Victor Graphics, Inc., Baltimore, MD
www.victorgraphics.com

Table of Contents

About the
Training Basics Series

■ ■

ASTD's *Training Basics* series recognizes and, in some ways, celebrates the fast-paced, ever-changing reality of organizations today. Jobs, roles, and expectations change quickly. One day you might be a network administrator or a process line manager, and the next day you might be asked to train 50 employees in basic computer skills or to instruct line workers in quality processes.

Where do you turn for help? The ASTD *Training Basics* series is designed to be your one-stop solution. The series takes a minimalist approach to your learning curve dilemma and presents only the information you need to be successful. Each book in the series guides you through key aspects of training: giving presentations, making the transition to the role of trainer, designing and delivering training, and evaluating training. The books in the series also include some advanced skills such as performance and basic business proficiencies.

The ASTD *Training Basics* series is the perfect tool for training and performance professionals looking for easy-to-understand materials that will prepare non-trainers to take on a training role. In addition, this series is the perfect reference tool for any trainer's bookshelf and a quick way to hone your existing skills. The titles currently planned for the series include:

- ▶ *Presentation Basics* (2003)
- ▶ *Trainer Basics* (2003)
- ▶ *Training Design Basics* (2003)
- ▶ *Facilitation Basics* (2004)
- ▶ *Performance Basics* (2004).

Preface

■ ■

The purpose of *Trainer Basics* is to help you to understand what training is and what it takes to be a trainer. Training builds upon many concepts and entails many activities, many of which may seem unrelated to each other. Even the term *training* has connotations that seem to be conflicting, if not mutually exclusive. For example, when I first started introducing myself as a trainer rather than a teacher (as I had been in a previous incarnation), one person asked me if I worked at Sea World! Well, training animals is a type of training, though it's not the topic of this book. But, you can see the problem.

Training encompasses the *science* of instructional design with its dependence on qualitative analysis and formal written objectives. It also includes the *art* of facilitation and presentation, which requires that one person utilize Hollywood-quality talent and ability to assist a group of disparate individuals as they try to master some new skill or acquire new knowledge.

Training is as old as the first child learning survival skills from its parents and as new as the computer age where e-learning allows today's learners to take advantage of the knowledge of the entire world from the convenience of their personal computers. It may or may not be education, it is or isn't the key to business productivity, and, when organizational times get tough, it may be deemed either expendable or irreplaceable.

Sometimes even seasoned trainers have a difficult time grasping the whole of training. Instead they specialize in fields such as instructional design, organization development, change management, or human performance improvement, and no longer even call themselves trainers.

How This Book Can Help You on Your Way

So, if you've found that you have a need for a book entitled *Trainer Basics,* you've begun an interesting journey, but one you won't need to travel alone. Together we'll explore the basics of what training is, where it came from, and where it may be going. We'll look at what makes a good trainer and the misconceptions that create poor ones. Along the way we'll discuss how adults learn, how good teachers teach, how proper planning ensures good training, and how we can determine if the training was not only good, but successful, which is often a very different thing. We'll meet designers, facilitators, performance technologists, instructional technologists, sales trainers, and for good measure, we'll learn to speak "trainer-speak," becoming fluent in concepts and terms such as knowledge management, competencies, blended learning, and job/task analysis.

This book strives to make it as easy as possible for you to understand and apply its lessons. Icons throughout the book help you identify key points:

What's Inside This Chapter

Each chapter opens with a short list—really a quick access guide—to introduce you to the rest of the chapter. If you are reading this book, you're probably in a hurry to get something done. You can use this section to identify the information it contains and, if you wish, skip ahead to the material that will be most useful to you.

Think About This

These little helpful reminders are like extra tools in your trainer's toolkit. Think of them as an extra layer of preparation of knowledge to build your confidence as a trainer.

Basic Rules

These rules cut to the chase. Although they are easy to remember, they are extremely important concepts for every trainer.

Noted

Sometimes a point or suggested practice needs some additional detail to help you understand the concept. Or, perhaps a little digression would be helpful to make a point. You will find these items under the "noted" icon.

Getting It Done

The final section of each chapter offers you a chance to practice some of the concepts discussed in the chapter and provides final tips and pointers to help you apply what you have learned.

Where to Go From Here

If this all sounds complicated, don't lose heart. The idea behind this book is to give you an overview of all that training is but in as simple a way as possible. Start with this book and then build your knowledge base by delving into the other books in this series and additional resources, as well. For now, master the basics and learn what you need to know for your specific role as a trainer.

No matter what reason you have for learning more about training—whether you are considering a career change or if you got "stuck" doing it because you know how to do your job better than anyone else—this book will be your first step, not just to being a trainer, but to being an outstanding one.

George M. Piskurich
December 2003

1

An Introduction to Training

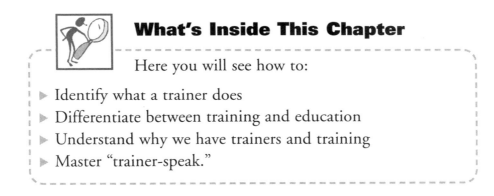

What's Inside This Chapter

Here you will see how to:

- ▶ Identify what a trainer does
- ▶ Differentiate between training and education
- ▶ Understand why we have trainers and training
- ▶ Master "trainer-speak."

So now you are a trainer. The first question you might ask is, "What is it that trainers actually do?" The answer may surprise you.

First, if you talk to enough trainers, you might believe that hardly anyone ever becomes a trainer on purpose. Just ask a few kids at the basketball court what they want to be when they grow up. How many kids do you suppose say "a trainer"? In fact, most people are not really sure what a trainer is or does, but—just for clarification—being a trainer does not mean you train lions for a three-ring circus.

Yet, you might think of trainers in terms of lion trainers. After all, trainers train people, not lions, to do amazing things.

Where Do Trainers Begin?

Most trainers come to the profession by rather disparate paths. Some trainers began as teachers, some as human resources professionals, others become trainers because they are subject matter experts (SMEs) asked to train new employees, and some became trainers through a job rotation process. It is easy to identify people in the workforce who came to training after careers as accountants, engineers, secretaries, computer operators, even actors, and stand-up comics.

If you are reading this book, perhaps you are one who has become a trainer by circumstance (you had certain knowledge that your organization wanted you to share with others) or perhaps by choice (you thought training would be fun to do and you wanted to make a career change). No matter. Whatever path you followed to get to the training profession, you are most likely interested in learning about the best way to succeed in this new profession.

This book will help you with that goal. In fact, this book will show you how to be not just a functioning trainer, but a competent and successful one whether your assignment is for a day, a year, or the rest of your career.

What Does a Trainer Do?

Many trainers end up as trainers because they have some specialized knowledge that needed to be shared with others. If you are asked to tell or show others what you know, then you can rightfully call yourself an SME.

Think About This

An SME is a person who through practice and experience has become expert at a skill set, task, job, or position that others need to learn. Although SMEs are not trainers, they are given training roles in many organizations every day. Nevertheless, the fact that you know something doesn't necessarily mean that you can teach it to others. Trainers can be SMEs if they have acquired both the subject matter proficiency and training skills. Trainers often use SMEs to help them learn about jobs, review parts of their training programs, and evaluate whether the training actually worked. In fact, SMEs are trainers' best resources, and smart trainers spend a great deal of time and energy building and maintaining excellent relationships with their SMEs.

On the other hand, if a supervisor asks you to teach someone new to the organization (often called a newbie by many trainers) immediately how to perform your job on a one-to-one basis, then you are an on-the-job trainer.

Lately, a whole new class of SME trainers skilled in computer programming has been created, thanks to the advent of e-learning. This new class of trainers is usually equipped with few training skills, yet their knowledge is in great demand, and training is a job this group is often asked to do.

For better or worse, all these new classes of trainers (SMEs, on-the-job trainers, and SME computer experts) must create training programs. This book will show you how to get started on the path to becoming an effective trainer, regardless of your prior career track.

Noted

Newbie *is a term used by trainers to indicate an employee who is new to the organization and needs training. A large percentage of the training carried out in most organizations is done for newbies.*

Other Trainer Jobs

In addition to standing up in front of a class with a flipchart imparting knowledge, trainers might do a number of other things including

- ▸ facilitating a focus group
- ▸ selling management on the concept of changing the way the entire organization learns.

This book will discuss most of these other trainer roles and even point you to additional resources that might be found in this book series and elsewhere. For the moment though, here's the top two things a trainer does:

1. classroom instruction (most likely as an SME)
2. on-the-job instruction.

Think About This

On-the-job training (OJT) refers to training that is conducted at or near the workstation rather than in a classroom. Such training can occur on a factory floor, in an office, or out in the field. The key characteristic of OJT is that it is done where the work is done, usually by a designated OJT trainer.

A Trainer Is . . .

Here is a humorous way to explain what a trainer does: A little boy brags to his sister that he taught his dog to whistle. When the sister listens and hears nothing she quizzes him on his statement, only to be told, "I said I taught him, I didn't say he learned!"

This story is a double-edged sword. It points out one of the great fallacies of training is that teaching is not learning. However, remember that it is still the learner's responsibility to learn, not the trainer's.

So what does a trainer really do? Simply put, a trainer tries to make it as easy as possible to learn. This is true whether you are standing in front of a classroom of new supervisors, working on the factory floor with a new machine operator who has that "deer in the headlights look," or sitting in front of a computer trying to figure out how you will explain your company's new defect-tracking system to group of engineers.

Training Versus Education

You may have noticed that the terms used so far in this book are training terms, such as trainer and learner. However, several terms—participant, trainee, student, pupil—are used in the profession that are taken to mean the same thing. If you think some of these terms sound like education terms, you would be right. In the long run, terminology does not matter, but names can affect perception, as shown in table 1-1.

A Short History of Training

Historically, training has been around as long as there have been people. Hundreds of years ago, one generation taught the next survival skills such as hunting, fishing, farming, and how to raise a family.

Picture in your mind an ancient flint knapper (a skilled person who makes stone tools from pieces of rock) patiently making tools outside his cave with two young

Basic Rule 1

A trainer cannot simply open a person's head and pour knowledge into it, although that would be a good trick. Moreover, a good trainer does not simply present information to learners and hope for the best. Good trainers are able to perform a feat that lies somewhere between the magic of instant understanding and the simple, factual presentation of material.

Table 1-1. Classification does make a difference.

Name	What the Name May Mean to You	What This Person May Actually Do
Attendee	Someone who shows up on time	Shows up, maybe
Audience	Someone who will laugh and clap for you	Pays attention, if entertained
Student	Someone who will behave like a child	Keeps quiet, takes notes, and answers questions if you ask first
Trainee	Someone who expects to be trained	Waits to be taught
Participant	Someone who takes an active role in training	Interacts with others and shares ideas when asked
Learner	Someone who is looking for value from your class	Shares ideas willingly and leaves with information that he or she can apply back in the workplace

apprentices looking on. Eventually, the knapper allows his apprentices to practice on pieces of flint as he guides them. Today this process would be called on-the-job training, or possibly one-to-one training. It is interesting to consider that this method is still the most effective form of training. Unfortunately, it is also the least efficient form of training.

Every training method that humans have created since has been an attempt to make training more efficient without losing any of the effectiveness of the flint knapper. This list of training methods includes classrooms, self-instruction, job aids, video, computer, satellites, e-learning, electronic performance support systems, and virtual reality, among others.

Basic Rule 2
When you think about it, the difference between training and education is simple. Training is all about gaining the knowledge or expertise to achieve some specific skill or goal. Education is more of a learning process that teaches students how to learn even more.

Think About This

A number of training concepts are covered by the term *apprenticeship*. They range from something as simple as a child learning through observation and practice to a skill that an adult has mastered to a formalized system in which a person learns a trade and becomes certified in it by working for and with a certified master. Some apprenticeship programs require monitored evaluations of the apprentice's skills such as internships in the medical field, whereas others are strictly a matter of time, usually measured in years, before the apprenticeship is completed. Good apprenticeships are based on the practice and exhibition of a set of commonly acknowledged skills that make up a job or profession.

Training Grows Up

The growth of factories didn't really change the idea of apprenticeship and learning by doing, but it did change the application of the concept. In the factories, it was still a master performer instructing an apprentice. The major difference was that in a large factory you had a number of master performers, some of whom were not quite as competent as others, teaching many apprentices, some of whom were not really suited to the task. Eventually, the concept of classrooms put these star performers in front of a number of these apprentices and, as you might surmise, even further from the ideal situation of a single master teaching a few apprentices.

Noted

All the training terms you see in this chapter (self-instruction, job aids, e-learning, performance support, and so on) fall under the heading of training methods. Training methods (or methodologies) are simply different ways that a trainer provides training. Several of these will be explored in subsequent chapters of this book, but be aware that each is unique unto itself and requires its own set of skills for a trainer to use effectively.

Training to the Rescue?

The training profession and all its theories and practices have been developed to overcome the problem of how to train many "apprentices" in an efficient and effective manner. It has led to the development of training aids as basic as flipcharts and as complex as computer-based training and simulations, plus a whole range of standardized practices including instructional systems development (ISD).

Instructional Design

The job of the instructional designer is to make a science out of training. The designer talks to the master performer but also observes the performance, talks to other performers, reads standard policies and procedures, discusses expectations with management, and pulls this information together into classroom content.

The instructional designer then creates a document that tells all trainers teaching a particular skill set what

Noted

Simulations as defined in this book can mean anything from a model of an actual machine that the learner can use for practice to more complex computer-driven simulators such as flight simulators to computer desktop simulations. The latter high-tech simulators rely on the learner to react to a virtual situation on the computer screen.

they need to teach and how to deliver the instruction effectively. This document, which may be called a lesson plan, an instructor guide, or any of a number of other terms, describes the content that must be taught, presents effective ways to teach it, and provides assessment tools that evaluate both the trainee and the training itself. The instructional designer, by definition, must be an expert at all these aspects of learning design. The concept of instructional design and the skills of the instructional designer will be discussed in more detail later in this book and in other books in this series.

Think About This

Instructional designers are trainers whose major responsibility is to create training programs. Usually they have been trained to do this because ISD is a specific series of procedures and processes used to create training programs that are both valid and effective. However, this is not always the case. Often SMEs with no ISD background are called upon to develop a training program as well as stand up before a class and deliver it. An instructional designer might be a stand-up trainer who delivers what he or she develops, but just as often the true instructional designer creates training that is delivered by others or that is delivered by a computer.

Basic Rule 3

Trying to train without understanding instructional design is like trying to play a game when no one knows the rules. In the end everyone loses.

Self-Directed Learning

Another way that training is done is through self-instruction (or self-directed learning), which is most often understood to mean a training program that the learners complete without the help of a trainer. These programs usually consist of a series of small sections, or chunks, each containing a step-by-step process that the learners follow at their own pace to master a piece of information. The lock-step design of self-instruction, as it was first developed, and the use of pre-computer machines to deliver it, caused it to be called *programmed instruction*. This term fell out of favor and is seldom used, but it is interesting that the advent of the computer reenergized the process considerably, though by another name, *e-learning*.

Self-Instruction

Self-directed learning is a term that is often used synonymously with self-instruction in the training world for the same type of trainer-less, do it at your own pace and time, lock-step training programs. However, in the academic environment, self-directed learning is a process in which learner choice is the key concept. Learners may choose what to learn, how to learn it, and how to evaluate the learning.

Noted

Learning specialist *is a new term being used in many companies in lieu of the word* trainer. *It refers to a position that is rather generic and as such does not have the same connotation as* trainer *(usually assumed to mean classroom instructor) or* instructional designer *(usually meaning a training materials development specialist). A learning specialist might spend all of his or her time analyzing, evaluating, creating programs, or teaching, or he or she may split time among all of these functions as well as others. The purpose of the title is to keep training practitioners from being "typecast" according to what they are called when, in fact, they perform a variety of different tasks.*

Academic research in self-directed learning has led to the concept of self-direction, which is seen as a character trait of learners. Self-direction, or self-directedness, has found a place in training as well, as a learner character trait that is necessary for some aspects of e-learning and for individualized development processes.

Trainers Today

Trainers, instructional designers, learning specialists, or whatever the practitioners of the various training disciplines might be called are looking to e-learning to provide that magic mix of effectiveness and efficiency that emulates the apprenticeship training of the past. They have taken on a great many tasks ranging from analyzing their company for training needs to evaluating the effectiveness of major organizational change interventions, but their primary responsibility is still to find ways to take their training to that level of one-to-one interaction that once existed.

And even with all this on their plates, trainers are trying to do more. They are asking for more involvement at the highest decision-making levels; looking for ways to have more influence on hiring practices, incentive plans, and staffing; and moving into diagnosis of both company and individual performance as they relate to organizational vision and objectives. They are saying, "We can do more than throw training at problems if you let us. We can help find the root causes of those problems, plan interventions that work at that root cause level, and even help management take advantage of performance opportunities to increase sales or gain market share." The days of the trainer as a classroom instructor are not and never will be gone, but today's busy trainer can and does do much, much more.

Think About This

There is an entire alphabet soup of acronyms for the various training technologies that are associated with computers, and they can get very confusing. Examples include CBT, CAI, CMI, WBT, and so forth. Many of them represent the same concept with slightly different twists, and many others have fallen out of usage entirely except that they appear in older books and magazine articles. If you need further definitions for these technology training acronyms, the best approach is to locate a book with a glossary that was written around the time when each was popular.

What Makes Good Training?

Structure is the key to good training. Just about anyone can get up before a group and talk about a familiar subject, and some people will learn from what they hear or see. However, to do more than just talk about a topic—to actually present it so your learners can learn it effectively—requires some thought, some self-preparation, some understanding of how people learn, and a great deal of planning. This planning constitutes the structuring of the training process and it is the reason for this book and hundreds like it.

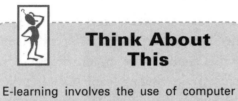

Think About This

E-learning involves the use of computer networks or electronic media to deliver training.

Structuring training means the creation of lesson plans that are built on proper analysis of your audience needs. It means handouts and other media for learners that help them to learn in addition to the assessment of how much learning actually took place during the class.

Structuring training is not easy. It takes time, energy, and money, but it ensures that learners get what they need to perform; moreover, it is presented in the most effective way possible, no matter who the trainer standing in front of the class. Here's an example:

> A rubber products company discovered that the way new workers were holding a rubber-cutting knife was creating too many rejected parts at the inspection stage of the process. The company discovered that the master cutters were providing the wrong instruction to the apprentices. When the company developed a structured OJT approach, it became apparent that several key techniques had been missing from the masters' instruction to the apprentices. Once these oversights were corrected, the product quality increased, and the reject problem ended.

Basic Rule 4

Good training is structured and consistent, no matter who or what does the training.

Trainer-Speak

"Trainer-speak" is very much the same as "doctor-speak" or "lawyer-speak," and any other professional "speak." It is the language that trainers use as part of their profession. Now that you are going to be a trainer, you must master some terminology.

This book will provide you with a good foundation in trainer-speak. You'll learn the basics of job analysis and other terms in this book, but you will need to continue your education beyond this book. Understanding the terminology is your entrance into the profession, so don't be afraid to ask questions if you don't understand a concept thrown out by another trainer.

As you go through this book you'll find many places where trainer-speak terms have more than one meaning or are not accepted by all practitioners. A good example of this is the still-evolving field of technology-based training, sometimes called e-learning, or distance learning, or Web-based learning. Sometimes those you train are called students, trainees, or learners. In the end it's all the same. In this book, those who are learning (the apprentices) are called learners, and you are the trainer (though such terms as instructors, facilitators, or training designers are often used).

Noted

Analysis can be a very complicated subject, but for now just note that this is a process trainers use to find out what their learners really need to learn.

Getting It Done

So far you've looked at what trainers do, how training and education may (or may not) differ as concepts, where training came from, and where it is today, and you've been introduced to trainer-speak. Based on what you've learned here and your personal experience, answer the questions in exercise 1-1 to help you consider these concepts on a more personal level.

Basic Rule 5

Being comfortable with your new trainer language is key to your success. Read this book. Ask questions. Learn about learning.

Exercise 1-1. Think like a trainer.

1. Trainers do many different things. List five different tasks you are performing or think you will perform as a trainer.

_____

_____

_____

_____

_____

2. You've seen the definition offered in this book, but use the space below for your own thoughts on how to differentiate training and education.

_____

_____

_____

_____

_____

3. Depending on whose definition you use, there are many different training methods. See how many you can list below.

_____

_____

_____

_____

_____

4. There are many indicators to show that a training program has been structured. The availability of learner materials is one such indicator. Think back to good training programs that you've attended (or good classes in school) and see how many other indicators of structure you can identify.

_____

_____

_____

_____

5. Learning trainer-speak is critical to your career as a trainer. Over the next week create a list of 10 or 15 trainer-speak terms that you hear, and try to find training definitions for them. You might want to use Angus Reynolds's *The Trainer's Dictionary* (Human Resource Development Press, 1993) or David Miles's *30-Second Encyclopedia of Learning and Performance* (AMACOM, 2003). Jot some trainer-speak terms down here:

Term	Definition

Now that you have delved into both the history and current state of training on a general basis, it's time to start looking at basics, and one of the most basic of the basics is understanding how the learners—adult learners, in particular—actually go about learning.

2

Adult Learning Theory

■ ■

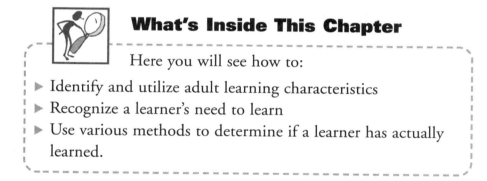

What's Inside This Chapter

Here you will see how to:

▶ Identify and utilize adult learning characteristics
▶ Recognize a learner's need to learn
▶ Use various methods to determine if a learner has actually learned.

No book about training (even a basic one) can be considered complete without a discussion of adult learning theory. Although this discussion can get very complicated (it is possible, after all, to get a doctoral degree in the subject of learning theory), this book will provide you with just enough background to help you become an effective trainer and understand the basic concepts. Many of the concepts presented here are common sense and probably reflect your own experiences as someone who has attended training classes. The trick you need to master is to take what you know and have experienced and what you are learning in this book and in other books, and apply all this information to your own classroom.

Adult Learner Characteristics

Every trainer you are likely too meet has read or knows about the seminal book by Malcolm Knowles (1980) about adult learning theory, *The Modern Practice of Adult Learning.* Knowles is credited with popularizing the terms *andragogy* (learning styles of adults) and *pedagogy* (learning styles of children).

Think About This

Malcolm Knowles suggested that there were important differences between the education of children versus the education (training) of adults. Among these are an awareness of the adult's need to bring his or her life experiences into the learning process and the importance of showing adults that they have a personal need to learn what was being presented. He termed this understanding of adult learning psychology and characteristics *andragogy*.

Here's a list of the most important points about learning derived from Knowles and other learning theorists. If you want to know more about this field of study, take a look at the Additional Resources section at the end of this book. If you pay close attention to the characteristics listed in table 2-1, your time as a trainer (however long or short) will be much more successful.

You should be aware that new research is frequently being published that expands our knowledge of how and why people learn. This field of study, which is termed cognitive science, looks at how the mind works and how humans structure new information, and remember and apply what they have learned. Extensive research is also being done into when learning actually takes place. When does the "eureka!" moment occur? Is it during a test? Or, is it when a skill is learned and demonstrated? All these issues are addressed in a discussion of the process of evaluating training later in this book.

Basic Rule 6

Good trainers pay attention to how adults learn. That way, they can create and deliver training that their audiences can relate to, increasing the probability that learning will occur.

Think About This

The study of pedagogy, or how children learn, has been going on for about as long as there have been children. Thousands of theories have been used, abused, discarded, and reinvented over the years. Some examples might include rote memorization (such as fraction tables), new math, phonics, classical education (such as Latin), Montessori schools, inquiry learning, guided discovery, and the latest attempts at school competency requirements. In the end, the main difference between andragogy and pedagogy may simply be the motivation that enables the learning.

Table 2-1. Characteristic of pedagogical and andragogical learners.

Learner Characteristic	Pedagogical	Andragogical
A dependent learner is . . .	✔	
A self-directed learner is . . .		✔
A learner who does not use experience as a resource is . . .	✔	
A learner who uses experience as a resource for him/herself and others is . . .		✔
A learner whose readiness to learn is directly related to age level and curriculum is . . .	✔	
A learner whose readiness to learn is developed from life's experience is . . .		✔
A learner whose orientation to learning is self-centered is . . .	✔	
A learner whose orientation to learning is task or problem centered is . . .		✔
A learner who is motivated by external rewards or punishments is . . .	✔	
A learner who is motivated by internal incentives and curiosity is . . .		✔

Adapted from Knowles, M.S. (1980). *The Modern Practice of Adult Learning*. Chicago: Follett.

The Need to Learn

Another question of interest to andragogists and pedagogists alike is why people learn. Research suggests that people only learn when they have a need to learn, no matter what the trainer does or how good the presentation. Adults are motivated to learn when they:

1. see the relevance of the training to their own life experience
2. have some control over their own learning experience
3. have a vast store of knowledge and experience from which to draw and apply to the current learning situation
4. regard growth in self-understanding equally as important as growth in learning
5. take an active part in the learning process
6. are in task- or experience-oriented learning situations
7. are in cooperative climates that encourage risk taking and experimentation (ASTD, 1998a).

For trainers, it is critical to know that a need to learn exists. Your attendees will not become learners unless this need is present. According to Knowles (1980), people respond to training based on external or internal reasons. For example, an external motivator might be a job promotion or better working conditions. An internal motivation (a more powerful motivator) might be self-esteem building, recognition by colleagues, or achievement.

Internal Motivation

Self-direction (or self-directedness) as a learner characteristic is where the principles of learning theory are manifest. Some learners simply have a strong internal need to learn. This may be a need to learn what they think is important to them or just to learn anything they can get their minds on.

Learners who have a strong internal need for learning do very well in training that is self-instructional in nature, such as computer-based training or asynchronous e-learning. Self-directed learning is also good for those who are internally motivated (more about this in chapter 6).

Research has shown that you can enhance the level of self-direction for most learners through interventions specifically designed for this purpose. These interventions allow the learners to recognize that they are already self-directed, and they

Think About This

Abraham Lincoln, Louis L'Amour, and Leonardo DaVinci are good examples of learners with ultra-high levels of self-direction. These individuals and many others, who are perhaps less well known, valued learning for its own sake. They overcame obstacles including social pressure, lack of resources, and even physical disabilities to pursue their own internal need to learn, not just what they were expected to learn, but what they wanted to learn, often contributing to the general store of human knowledge by doing so.

provide an opportunity to succeed at a small but recognizable self-directed learning activity. They also provide a support system that is available for the learners until they become comfortable with learning on their own. The interventions may be classroom based, part of a development system and facilitated by a supervisor, or an introduction to an e-learning process (Huey B. Long and Associates, 1989; 1990; 1992). It's important to remember these interventions if you ever find yourself embarking on a voyage into the sometimes rough waters of e-learning, or if your organization already has an e-learning system going, but it's not going well.

You would think that every trainer would prefer to work with learners who have a high internal need to learn. It would seem that all you need to do is provide the proper content, and the learner will do the rest. To some extent, this assumption is true, but if you misjudge what content the learner needs, you can easily discourage the learning process. In addition, the internally motivated learner can easily be distracted by superfluous or tangential information because he or she is interested in *all* sorts of information, not just what is relevant to the learning objectives.

External Motivators

As you might expect, a learning need brought about by something happening outside the learner is called an *external need*. This category includes the need for learning required for a certification or a degree. Sometimes an employer requires new-product training, supervisory training, or safety training. The learner may have little or no internal need for the subject matter, but the need to learn is still there.

Most pedagogical learning is externally motivated, with the students needing to learn to earn good grades, to make their parents happy, or to graduate from school, which shades into an internal need as well, though the actual learning is still externally motivated.

WIIFM

"What's in it for me?" (WIIFM) is a key phrase for trainers and the preeminent motivator for most human activity. The WIIFM mentality helps learners translate the external need into an internal need, even if that need is only to get this training over with and pass the test. This motivator is exemplified by the student who really has no internal need to learn algebra but internalizes the need as a need to graduate. Without this change from an externally motivated need to an internal one, your learners will not learn (figure 2-1).

More on Motivation

Most often the need to learn is some combination of internal and external needs. For example, a learner may have an internal motivation to learn supervisory skills because he or she has been given a new job title. The concept of team building, however, may be a subject that holds little personal interest. Yet, the external driver (the fact that this is part of the supervisory program) ensures that this part of the training program is completed.

Figure 2-1. The importance of motivating learners.

Think About This

WIIFM is perhaps the most important aspect of any training program. If you can't show your learners that your program will benefit them, then it's unlikely to be a success. There are many kinds of WIIFMs and about as many ways to present them. Two suggested methods are to articulate clearly the WIIFM to learners: Either you'd better know the WIIFM yourself so that you can emphasize it for the learners, or you'll have to take time to guide the learners so they can discover the WIIFM themselves. The second approach requires more time but provides you with better motivated learners.

Your job as a trainer is to discover as much as you can about your learners' learning needs and take advantage of that knowledge by helping them internalize the need for training you are presenting.

How Do You Know Your Learners Actually Learned?

Another aspect of adult learning theory is the question of how do you know that a learner has learned the material presented. As a trainer, it is important for you to know what and how much of the presented material was retained and applied back in the workplace.

Many types of testing exist. Paper-and-pencil evaluations are familiar to everyone. You will find as you discover more about training that a whole field of study is devoted to the taking and giving of tests. Giving tests is much more complicated than just thinking up hard questions. A test that truly measures if your learners have learned what you hoped they would is an integrated part of your training planning or what was referred to earlier as your instructional design. It's not just an afterthought or something you create the day before you give it to your learners.

Basic Rule 7

Good trainers pay attention to why adults want to learn. Failure to do so can often lead to training that no one really wants or can use.

Think About This

There is much more to the study of learning retention than first meets the eye. Research scientists are studying the learning process at the biochemical level, but trainers usually concentrate on other aspects of learning: learning curves, mnemonics, mind mapping, job aids as retention refreshers and electronic performance support systems (EPSS), and a concept called just-in-time training (JIT). In JIT you try to deliver the training just before the learner needs to use it, thus making the actual use of it self-reinforcing, thereby increasing retention dramatically. Although learning retention is frequently a topic of discussion and focus, few trainers take the time to measure retention in their learners, which is unfortunate because it is a great indicator of the success of training programs.

Adult learning theory has provided other indicators that can be used by trainers to show that learning has occurred and has been retained. You'll probably hear many theories concerning how much knowledge is lost and how soon that knowledge is lost after training and perhaps even more information on what can be done to enhance retention. Mnemonics, mind maps, job aids, and refresher training are all

Noted

"Today, with the continued emphasis on showing a real return on the training investment, it is essential that performance improvement specialists, trainers, and especially technical trainers be able to document the skill competency levels of employees who complete training. One method for ensuring that a 'skills transfer' takes place is for training and performance professionals to follow a model that encompasses identification, demonstration, coaching, and assessment of newly acquired job skills" (ASTD, 1998b). This model evaluates whether the knowledge and skills that were learned in the training were applied when the learner returned to the job. Unlike measures of retention, trainers often do gather data on transfer, but it is a difficult task, as you will see when this concept is explored in more detail.

concepts related to the process of retention, though in the final analysis perhaps the expression "Use it or lose it" is a good rule of thumb.

Tests have been the traditional means for measuring learning retention, although there are many other ways of evaluating learning. Just remember that tests can be a valid indicator of learning, but if not used properly, they are poor indicators of retained knowledge. You'll read more about tests and other forms of learner evaluation in chapter 5.

Learn by Doing

Humans learn best by doing. Many trainers believe that the only way someone is going to learn a skill is by doing it him- or herself either in a real or a simulated environment. In addition, plenty of structured and easily available learning resources are integral to this approach without the benefit of a trainer standing over the learner's shoulder.

Think About This

Here are a few more terms to add to your trainer-speak vocabulary:

- *Mnemonics* are memory prompts in various forms such as rhymes or visualizations that facilitate retention of facts or even concepts. For example, "Every Good Boy Does Fine" is a mnemonic for remembering the musical notes (E, G, B, D, F) that are on the lines of the treble clef scale.
- *Mind maps* are the recording and formatting of information in ways that go beyond the normal paragraphs in order to create constructs with key points that are easier to retain.
- *Job aids* link training to practice and increase retention by providing facts or procedures that require reinforcement on the job.
- *Refresher training* is usually a yearly training intervention in which the key points of training that had been done earlier are restated and reinforced.
- *Coaching* allows learners to receive reinforcement and so retain information through an individual who helps them master skills while they are on the job.
- *EPSS* is an electronic and usually more complex form of a job aid that the learners can refer to on the job for reinforcement.

Pedagogists have been using this process for years and have termed it *discovery learning*. The indicator of learning in this method is the learner's ability to do something after the training that he or she could not do before. This change in ability often is more intellectual than physical and, therefore, is harder to measure. For example, you might build your skills as a presenter through discovery by learning how to think on your feet during arguments. The skill change is in your facilitation ability, but it is a mental change occurring internally that has caused it.

Other Adult Learning Processes

You will surely encounter other adult learning theories as you learn more about training. Two are introduced here.

Competency-Based Training

Many trainers believe that competency-based training is the best way to build learner skills. They hold that each job or task is made up of competencies that are critical to a process. Because each competency builds on the next, each must be mastered by all learners who have a need for the particular skill. These competencies are best exemplified by the knowledge and skills of the master performer. By observing what

Think About This

Pedagogists have been using the concepts of discovery, as well as guided discovery and inquiry, to involve their students more fully in the learning process for years. These concepts are similar but not quite the same. In discovery learning the learner starts with a basic objective but is on his or her own from there to use learning resources to master the objective. In guided discovery the teacher provides a bit more guidance, perhaps even a second level of objectives or a learning contract to help focus the learner's learning. In inquiry, even the objectives are missing, and the learners are on their own to define what it is they need to learn and how to go about it. Trainers tend to lean toward the discovery and guided-discovery methods when they attempt these types of learner involvement processes in their training programs.

Basic Rule 8

Your training is not successful unless your learners have actually learned what you intended them to learn. Assessment is necessary to find this out.

the master performer does, the trainer can develop a list of these competencies and then use the list to train new learners to act like master performers.

Accelerated Learning

Another area of adult learning considers how trainers can train their learners faster and to retain more. This practice is known as accelerated learning.

Accelerated learning is a series of learning strategies designed to increase learning speed and retention. Accelerated learning may include the use of visuals, games, simulations, storytelling, metaphors, and learner involvement techniques, as well as job performance techniques such as teaching others and self-assessment.

Noted

What is a job? In the training profession, you must be aware that there are varying levels of complexity to jobs. It falls to you as a trainer to define a job in terms of competencies and at least one level of tasks. Your HR department often supplies job descriptions that you can analyze and build upon to create a list of competencies that constitute a job. It's amazing that a simple three-letter word such as job can create so much confusion and lead to so many repercussions if not defined carefully.

A task is somewhat easier to define than a job. Tasks are the things that make up a job. However, a given job may be associated with several layers of tasks. A job usually consists of one or main tasks, each of which, in turn is composed of one or more subtasks, and on it goes. Although jobs and layers of tasks are sometimes confusing, they are critical to the training process as you will see in the next chapter, which addresses task analysis.

Getting It Done

In this chapter you explored the sometimes confusing concept of adult learning theory. You should now know why understanding how adults learn is important to you as a trainer, how to capitalize on your learners' need to learn, and be aware of some ways to measure learning. Complete exercise 2-1 to review these concepts in a more self-directed method.

Exercise 2-1. Applying principles of adult learning to the training field.

1. Think about yourself and what you prefer in your learning processes as an adult, compared to how you learned back when you were in school or how your own children like to learn. Create your own list to compare adult learning characteristics to those of a child. Are they different or pretty much the same? How can you use these differences when you teach adults?

Adult Learning Characteristics	Child Learning Characteristics

2. The next time you are in a class or other training situation, talk to your learning colleagues about why they are there, that is, what learning need brought them to class. Is the training helping them to meet their needs? If not, how might you structure the training so it would?

3. Do you assess whether your learners have actually learned? If so, how do you determine it? What other indicators might you use?

4. Use the Web or any other easily accessible resource to find out more about accelerated learning. List five accelerated learning methods or concepts below. How might you use these in your own training?

_____

_____

_____

_____

_____

5. Explaining WIIFM is critical to helping adults learn. Consider the training programs you have attended, and record below the various ways instructors have presented WIIFM in them.

The next chapter gets into the real work of being a trainer, and it begins with what is known as task analysis.

3

Analyzing Training Needs

What's Inside This Chapter

Here you will see how to:

▶ Identify reasons for doing analysis
▶ Assess various analysis tools and techniques
▶ Describe the importance of obtaining time to do analysis
▶ Integrate the various aspects of analysis into a system.

This chapter is entitled "Analyzing Training Needs," but it could just as easily been entitled "Assessing Training Needs," or "Analyzing Learning Needs." The terms *analysis* and *assessment* are often used interchangeably by trainers. However, the term used in this book is *training analysis*. Part of the reason for this convention is that it will cut down on the level of confusion concerning the topic. (Don't worry; confusion is always rampant for new trainers when they try to understand analysis.) The other reason for this convention, which will be discussed later, is that the word *assessment* is often used to mean *evaluation*.

The Foundation of Training

Training analysis is the foundation of any successful training. Without analysis your training program and possibly your new career would probably collapse. This chapter will introduce you to the basics of training analysis, including some terminology specific to this field. Terminology can be a big problem for those new to the training profession, but it's important to become familiar with the language of analysis. As discussed in chapter 1, getting comfortable with trainer-speak is important to your development as a trainer.

The Basics of Training Analysis

For now, you should probably just remember that there's not much difference between a training analysis, a training needs assessment, a needs analysis, or, for that matter, between performance analysis or a training assessment.

Why Analyze?

Analysis is done for one reason—to find out what your learners need to know to be successful. It's important to remember, though, that training is but one option among myriad interventions that might be the answer to fill a performance gap. Nevertheless, this book is dedicated to the basics of training, so the emphasis is on training interventions that can help your learners succeed in the workplace.

The Analysis Process

As a trainer, you do analysis to determine the training needs of an organization, a department, or an individual. For this book, just assume that your training need is the same as learning need and will require you to come up with some type of intervention to provide needed knowledge, skills, or expertise.

First, think about whom you are trying to serve with your training intervention. Is it your entire organization, just a department, or an individual? For your analysis, you need to think in terms of big-group training and small-group training.

Basic Rule 9
Don't spend a great deal of time worrying about the terminology that you hear. Training analysis is the same whether you call it needs assessment or needs analysis.

Think About This

Intervention is a general term for any process that a trainer implements. The term was first used by organization development (OD) specialists to differentiate what they implemented from training. Later it was picked up by human performance improvement (HPI) practitioners and has become a basic term in their discipline. Trainers now use the term as well, so you'll often run across it. It's used to indicate that what the trainers are implementing is not necessarily a classroom program, which is what most people think of when they hear the term *training.*

Non-classroom interventions related to training include mentoring, job aids, and some aspects of e-learning. Those related more closely to performance technology might include changes in organizational structure, changes in compensation or incentive programs, even new chairs for workers to sit on that are more ergonomic and better suited to their particular work space.

Big-Group Training. If you analyze the training needs of an organization, you are taking on a larger task that may require training everyone in the organization to ensure that goals are met or a set of stated mission objectives is met. Training programs for organizations might include such training as:

- ▶ new employee orientation programs
- ▶ diversity training
- ▶ supervisory or management training
- ▶ ethics training.

If you are doing training in these big-group areas, then you might use the terms *training analysis, training assessment, needs assessment,* or *training needs assessment.*

A trainer uses big-group training analysis to set a general path that the proposed training will take and uses the results of analysis to justify training.

Small-Group Training. You might need to analyze the training needs of smaller groups in the organization, such as a department or a work group. Training needs of these groups can include concepts such as product knowledge, technical training on how to run a machine or complete a certain manufacturing process, sales training, customer service, communications skills, teamwork, and even specific professional development training.

Analysis for these jobs often falls under the categories of learning analysis or job/task analysis and can also be part of a performance analysis. You might want to call this small-group analysis just to differentiate it from the big-group variety.

Noted

A performance analysis is one of the techniques used in a discipline known as performance technology. It's a newer form of analysis and looks either at individual or group performance rather than the need for training.

Audience Analysis

Audience analysis, which is also called learner analysis or participant analysis, examines common learning characteristics of all the learners in a small group. Table 3-1 lists some aspects of that you might analyze in an audience analysis.

Table 3-1. Characteristics of the training audience you may want to analyze.

Analyze?	Audience Characteristic
☐	Age
☐	Sex
☐	Reading level
☐	Life experience
☐	Experience in current job or others related to training
☐	Current job performance
☐	Language differences
☐	Cultural differences
☐	Motivation for taking training
☐	Formal education
☐	Hobbies
☐	Company training programs that have already been attended
☐	Geographic location(s)
☐	Prerequisite knowledge and skills that learners have (or do not have)

Basic Rule 10

You must do analysis. Without it you cannot be sure that you are providing the training that your learners need.

Note that to understand learner characteristics fully, audience analysis may extend all the way down to the level of a single learner, in which case it is often called an *individual needs assessment.*

Individual needs assessments are not performed as commonly as big- and small-group analysis, but they are becoming more practical in today's environment of Web-based training, assessment technologies, and individualized development. Individual needs assessment can also be called prescriptive learning analysis because it usually ends up with a plan or prescription for an individual that is used both to bring under-developed skills up to a higher level and to develop new skills that will lead to a longer-range goal, such as a promotion or even a new position.

How to Do Analysis—Tools and Techniques

Analysis tools abound, and you should be able to find an analysis tool for just about any purpose, ranging from assessing an individual's readiness to learn to analyzing how closely an organization complies with its mission statement. (See the Additional Resources section for more on analysis.) ASTD offers a number of resources on the

Think About This

Web-based training or assessment (or most anything else with *Web* in front of it) should mean that access to the process is obtained through the World Wide Web and a Web browser. However, in training it may also mean, as in the case of assessment technology, that access is through the company's intranet. This means very little to trainers, as long as their trainees have the technology and know how to use it. Trainers are more interested in what their trainees do when they get there rather than how they got there. Of course, if the technology or the learners' ability to use it is in question the trainers should be very interested in the how the learners accessed the training as well.

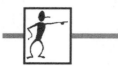

Noted

Individualized development is a system for developing employees in which the employee and his or her supervisor are responsible for deciding what development must occur and for finding the learning resources to make it happen.

subject. You can also find Web-based assessment instruments that should be useful to you. The second book in this series, *Training Design Basics* (Carliner, 2003), is also a good resource for your analysis education.

If you can use an off-the-shelf tool or even a template from a book that requires little or no modification, you'll save a great deal of time. If, however, you must create your own assessment tool, the next sections describe some techniques to get the information you need to provide successful training.

If you're going to create and implement your own training analysis tools, you may wish to consider some of the alternatives listed here.

Interviews

The interview technique, as the name implies, involves basically talking with people and asking them questions. Interviews can be conducted face to face, on the phone, or even over the Web. It's a good idea to plan the questions in advance and, better still, to send your interviewees a copy of the questions ahead of time. You'll want to take plenty of notes on what they say and possibly even use a tape recorder if it isn't too intrusive.

Think About This

Trainers use the term *off-the-shelf* to mean any program or tool that has been created for general use by all organizations and that can be purchased, ready to use, from a supplier. Off-the-shelf training programs or trainer tools require much less time than the time it takes to develop your own renditions, but if off-the-shelf processes don't fit the organization's needs and culture they are seldom worth the price, no matter how low.

The key issues here are to make sure that you are asking the right people the right questions and that you follow up on their answers as this is what makes an interview a stronger analysis technique than a questionnaire.

Questionnaire

Questionnaires are most useful when you have a limited amount of time (interviews require a fair bit of time) or when you want to hear from a large number of learners. There's an art to developing a good questionnaire, and it takes some practice. For example, you should use a mixture of both open- and closed-ended questions.

One problem with questionnaires is that the return rate is usually quite small; 15 to 20 percent should be at the high end of your expectations. Another drawback is that you will need to use an interview or some other technique if you have follow-up questions or if you didn't understand what your subjects were saying.

Focus Group

The method of choice for those in the marketing field, focus groups are also a great analysis technique for trainers. By bringing a small group of people together and having them react to each other's comments and ideas, you can get in-depth and often unique information concerning training needs that no other technique will provide.

You need to choose your group carefully, basing your mix on what you hope to find out, and it's best if you have a note taker or at least a tape recorder, because once focus groups get rolling, they tend to put out information at a fast and furious pace. Some trainers prefer to have an assistant lead the group while the trainer takes notes about what to follow up on with specific people in the group. You need to keep good control over your focus groups so they don't stray from your purpose or become a big gripe session.

Observation

Observations are usually a good follow-up analysis technique, often used to validate training needs that you have already identified. This technique is also used extensively in competency-based training, and in both job analysis and performance analysis, which are discussed later. One of the problems with observation is that people seldom do what they really do when they know someone is watching. That's why observation is a better follow-up technique as you can ask questions concerning how and why someone is doing something if you already have an idea of what you should be observing.

Research

Research is one of the most underused analysis techniques. Most organizations have thousands of pages of printed material, which, if analyzed well, can point out many training needs. For example, policy and procedure manuals can tell you the way things should be done, and through observation you can see if that is the way they are done. The problem with research is that it's really boring, certainly not as much fun as visiting a factory floor or holding an interview. However, browsing through company documents can help narrow the focus of your analysis quickly, once again saving both the time and the cost of doing interviews or distributing questionnaires.

Analysis—It Takes Time

Good analysis takes time and, as you well know, time is something no one has much of these days. Nevertheless, don't give this part of your job short shrift. Analysis is the foundation of training. You can create the most successful and enjoyable training and even get great evaluations and still fail at being a trainer because your learners did not learn what was needed for your organization or that individual to be successful. Proper analysis guards against this possibility by allowing you to determine what training is important to achieve the training goal you are trying to accomplish.

So What's the Problem?

You should never start a journey in a car unless you know where you are headed. The same common sense applies to training. However, planning and thinking takes time. You may have trouble convincing some in your organization (oftentimes management) that analysis is necessary. Management is simply looking for results as quickly and cheaply as possible.

Management does have a point, though. You can analyze anything too much. Ever heard of the term *analysis paralysis?* A good trainer needs to know when the time has come to stop analyzing and start creating training. You need to strike a balance between getting enough analysis done and getting the training out. It's a high-wire act and sometimes you fall, but you can create a net by helping your clients, that is, the people you are developing training for, to see the importance of analysis.

Basic Rule 11

Good analysis always takes more time, but don't over-analyze the problem. Too much analysis is just as bad as too little analysis.

Analysis As a System

One of the reasons analysis takes so much time is that it is not a singular process, but a system consisting of three steps. Each aspect of an analysis system is based on the conclusions made from the information gathered in the previous step. You may not have the need or the time to create an entire analysis system, but it may help you understand the concept a little better if you see how each step in such a system builds upon the previous one.

Analysis Step 1

The first step in an analysis system is to analyze big-group training needs. Interviews, focus groups, and other techniques discussed earlier are critical to this step. One of these analysis tools should provide you with some general organizational needs for training and some clues as to the needs at small-group levels.

Think About This

Here is a good training story that may help you with the analysis part of your job. A trainer was told by a data entry manager that his department needed training because of poor typing skills. Instead of analysis, the trainer assumed the manager knew the cause of the problem. The trainer spent a few weeks developing great keyboard skills training, and he trained 90 employees using the training program he wrote. A month later, the manager complained to the trainer that the training did not work.

Discouraged and disheartened the trainer happened to talk to someone who had gone through his class. The learner had liked the class and reported a dramatic improvement in keyboard skills. The real problem, however, the learner said, was that the software they were using was inadequate for the job.

Analysis Step 2

Next, analyze your small-group training needs. Because there may be many small groups in an organization, this step may require substantial time. You can improve your efficiency by starting to create training programs to meet big-group needs while you are conducting small-group needs analysis. Or, you can deal with one or more training issues that emerged from your first small-group analysis. The clues from your big-group analysis can help you focus your small-group analysis somewhat, but you'll simply need to work your way through the rest of the process to get the information you need.

This is the level at which most of your training programs will become apparent, and where you will deal with job skills and the needs of work groups.

Analysis Step 3

The third step is to analyze individual training needs. This is where you can really do some efficient training because you can use your analysis skills to help you prescribe just the right training for just the right person, without waste and without redundancy. By analyzing individual needs you can look for learning that is common for people across the organization and so focus your training development on programs that will help the most people do the best job. The problem with this step, as with analysis in general, is that it takes time—and lots of it! Plan to attempt it slowly, building the process as you complete the work on the needs indicated in steps 1 and 2 of your system.

The Reality of Analysis

In the real world, you often need to cut short your analysis system. Correlate and assign priorities to all the training needs. For example, you may discover that there is an obvious training need and create a program to address that need first. (Sometimes another corporate analysis may help you, and it is okay to use that data for a large training goal.) Then, as you dig deeper, you become more able to develop

Basic Rule 12

If you need to jumpstart your training, do a focused analysis on one specific area of need instead of a general analysis to determine all needs.

the training necessary to meet secondary needs. Perhaps you don't have the advantage of an already completed analysis, but you can do a highly focused mini-analysis to determine a couple of definite training needs and begin working on those as you plan and implement your analysis system.

What if you are told to create a training program and not given the time or the budget to do analysis? Here a few tactics that will help you get around this impasse:

▶ Ask the person requesting the training about the analysis that revealed the training need and what it said. This information will give you some clue what to cover and why. If you do not get a good answer here, then you have a bigger problem in that the foundational analysis might never have been done. In that case you'll need to start at the beginning with your own general analysis of training needs.

▶ Complete a small-group analysis of your learners to lay the foundation for the training intervention you intend to do. You may have to do some job analysis, task analysis, learner analysis, or delivery analysis, but a good start is knowing your overall training need.

▶ Create a first draft of objectives for your training based on discussions with SMEs, then send these objectives to management and other interested groups to make sure you are on the right track in addressing a critical need.

Noted

If you need a quick guide to analysis types, here it is:
- Job analysis: *A trainer analyzes a job (using whatever definition has been decided upon for a job) to determine the tasks that make up the job.*
- Task analysis: *These tasks are analyzed further to determine the skill and knowledge components of each task.*
- Learner analysis: *This analysis is used to find out the characteristics of the trainees you are going to train so you can use these characteristics to create training that the trainees will relate to.*
- Delivery analysis: *Such an analysis helps you determine which training method will be the most effective and efficient for your training program.*

Getting It Done

This chapter discussed the importance of doing analysis first to determine training needs and to gather more information on audience characteristics, delivery possibilities, and job tasks that can help you in creating a training program. Use exercise 3-1 to help you practice some of these analytical processes.

Exercise 3-1. Taking another look at training analysis.

1. List at least three good reasons for doing analysis.

_____

_____

_____

2. List five different types of analysis discussed in this chapter and each one's purpose.

Type of Analysis	Purpose

3. Using your analysis list from question 2 and the list of analysis techniques in the chapter, create a list of techniques that you feel would work best for the various analysis types.

Type of Analysis	Technique That Would Work Best

4. Using a real-life training situation that you are involved in (or a fictitious one if you don't have a real one), write a memo to the appropriate manager explaining why you require the time and resources to do a thorough training analysis.

5. Choose two Web-based assessment tools and compare their characteristics and usefulness to your organization. You can find suppliers of these tools on the ASTD Website (www.ASTD.org), or you can use an Internet search engine.

Assessment Tool #1: _____

_____

_____

_____

_____

Assessment Tool #2: _____

_____

_____

_____

_____

After you have completed your analysis, the next step in this process is the creation of good learning objectives based on the results of your analysis—the subject of the next chapter.

4

The Importance
of Learning Objectives

■ ■

What's Inside This Chapter

Here you will see how to:
▶ Create training objectives from your analysis
▶ Structure objectives from higher levels to lower (simpler) levels
▶ Write objectives that can be used effectively by your learners
▶ Use objectives to create effective training programs.

A lack of objectives is the main reason behind failed training. It is that simple. If you've ever been in a training class that lacked objectives, you know why this statement is true.

Why Bother With Objectives?

There is a school of thought that says learning, not objectives, is what matters. However, it makes more sense to consider that you will be more successful if you know what your learner needs to learn and you provide that training.

Basic Rule 13

Training that does not include objectives is not training, it is more a quiz show where the learners try to guess what it is that they should know.

Objectives have a long history in training. One of the main reasons trainers have problems with objectives is that useful ones are difficult to create. Yet it is essential that your learner knows what is necessary to learn and what information is important. For example, a classroom teacher is more effective if he or she says, "Here's your list of objectives. When you've mastered these you will have learned what you need for this program," instead of, "If you listen, you'll know what you need to learn."

Where Do Objectives Come From?

Good objectives are the result of your analysis of training needs. This is why analysis is so important. No matter what type of analysis you have chosen to create, you should be able to write solid objectives. The level of the objective should match the level of the analysis.

For example, if you have done a training analysis, you should create objectives that relate directly to the training needs of the organization. Note that you are not always going to create formal objectives at the organizational level. Your organization might be better served if you provide simpler *learning goals.* For example, here are a couple examples of effective learning goals:

▸ Create a workforce that is more knowledgeable of organizational policies and procedures.
▸ Enhance the ability of employees to use electronic technology properly in day-to-day operations.

Objectives for the Learner

Objectives at the learner level are called performance objectives. They are usually based on analysis processes such as a job or task analysis. Remember that to get to the job analysis level, you will also need analysis from a higher, organizational level in accordance with your analysis system (chapter 3).

Think About This

Performance objectives are also often called behavioral objectives because they have a behavioral verb as an integral part of them. The term *behavioral objective* is often preferred because it can better define all types of objectives. If this is the case, the term *performance objective* is used to describe an objective based on an actual performance of a task rather than a gathering of knowledge, which is what most objectives relate to. Some trainers use the term *knowledge objective* to tag that type of objective. So, behavioral objectives have a behavioral verb (among other things) and can be subdivided into knowledge objectives that deal with the acquisition of information and performance objectives that deal with the exhibition of a skill. Some trainers like this approach, but many other trainers still call them all performance objectives.

For example, your learning objective might be something like "Identify the four cogs that need to be replaced when the widget machine flashes an amber light." If done correctly, you can trace this objective the whole way back to the mission statement, goals, and needs of the entire organization.

How to Structure Objectives

Trainers can write objectives from any phase of the analysis process. From a big-group analysis, you create objectives that provide the basis for all objectives and are mainly for organization-wide training needs. On the other hand, objectives written from a small-group analysis provide detailed concepts and skills that will be taught in a single class or group of classes. As noted earlier, job and task analysis provides objectives at the learner level.

Basic Rule 14

If you cannot relate your objectives directly back to training analysis, something is really wrong. Go back and try it again.

Constructing a Training Objective

Here is a sample big-group training objective: Provide the company with a work-force that serves customer needs and produces world-class quality products.

This big-group goal is supported by many other objectives that drill down to the level of the individual. For example this large goal might be supported by the following objectives:

> ▶ The employees will be able to explain the company's customer service goal statement.
> ▶ The employees will utilize the five-step method for creating a high-quality product in each aspect of their job.

Objectives Versus Goals

Higher-level objectives are more akin to goals. It does not matter what you call these statements as long as you understand how to use and construct them. In the true sense of the training profession, a "real" objective is written from a learner's perspective, and it includes observable or measurable behaviors. In the end, the most useful objectives are ones that work and produce results.

How to Write Objectives

There is no single way to write objectives. Robert Mager (1975), one of the pioneers of constructing objectives, developed a four-part process for creating objectives that (1) are learner centered and include (2) a behavioral verb, (3) conditions, and (4) criteria for success, as shown in table 4-1. Some other experts, though, say it is a three- or even two-part process.

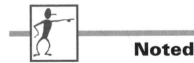

Noted

Mager's classic book on objectives, Preparing Instructional Objectives *(1975), has been the bible on objective-writing for many years. It is succinct, easy to read, and understandable. It should be on every trainer's bookshelf. Mager's four-part approach to writing proper objectives has taken some hits over the years, but for a new trainer who's writing objectives for the first time, they are golden. They'll keep you out of trouble as you learn through practice to write objectives your learners can really use.*

Table 4-1. Writing three-part learning objectives.

The Behavior	The Criterion	The Conditions
An observable, measurable behavior: State this behavior using an action verb such as *install, type, describe,* or *state.* Avoid words like *know, understand, appreciate,* and *inform* for the tasks because knowing, understanding, and appreciating (and terms like them) cannot be measured. Usually, each task identified in the needs analysis becomes an objective (with alterations resulting from your review of this list).	*Conditions under which the task should be performed:* This part describes any situations that should be considered when measuring the goal, such as the availability of reference materials when users perform a task. Most frequently, the conditions state whether learners can have access to resources such as a textbook while performing the task.	*Level of acceptable performance:* This describes the extent to which the objective must be achieved to be considered complete, such as "without errors." The level of acceptable performance is assumed to be 100 percent, unless stated otherwise.
↓	↓	↓
"Label all documents classified as confidential with the word 'Confidential' in the top margin . . .	. . . using the automatic header and footer function of the word processor . . .	. . . with 100 percent accuracy (both in placing the warning and remembering to use it)."

Adapted from Carliner, S. (2003). *Training Design Basics.* Alexandria, VA: ASTD; and Mager, R. (1975). *Preparing Instructional Objectives.* Belmont, CA: Pitman Learning Inc.

Mager believes that each learning objective, in addition to being learner centered, should consist of

▶ *a behavior:* the verb you pick to let the learners know what they need to do (list, explain, analyze, construct, run, and so forth)

▶ *the criteria:* the way that you will evaluate performance (every time, at an 80 percent level, with no errors, and so forth)

▶ *the conditions:* how the trainee will perform the task (in the classroom, on a test, in the field, without notes, and so forth).

Table 4-2 lists various behaviors that are both behavioral and measurable. They are often referred to as behavioral verbs. This list is not exhaustive, but it will provide you with a starting point to create your own objectives.

Table 4-2. Behavioral verbs.

Knowledge	Comprehension	Application	Analysis	Synthesis	Evaluation
Count	Associate	Apply	Order	Arrange	Appraise
Define	Compare	Calculate	Group	Combine	Assess
Draw	Compute	Classify	Translate	Construct	Critique
Identify	Contrast	Complete	Transform	Create	Determine
Indicate	Describe	Demonstrate	Analyze	Design	Evaluate
List	Differentiate	Employ	Detect	Develop	Grade
Name	Discuss	Examine	Explain	Formulate	Judge
Point	Distinguish	Illustrate	Infer	Generalize	Measure
Quote	Estimate	Practice	Separate	Integrate	Rank
Recognize	Extrapolate	Relate	Summarize	Organize	Rate
Recall	Interpret	Solve	Construct	Plan	Select
Recite	Interpolate	Use		Prepare	Test
Read	Predict	Utilize		Prescribe	Recommend
Record	Translate			Produce	
Repeat				Propose	
State				Specify	
Tabulate					
Trace					
Write					

Some trainers want to make sure that all three elements of objectives (behavior, criteria, conditions) are in all objectives they write. But, depending on your particular training situation you may determine that the conditions and even the criteria are understood. In such cases, you don't have to write these elements explicitly into your

Think About This

The best way to make sure your objectives are learner centered is to start each one with the phrase, "The learner will be able to . . . ." This phrasing is cumbersome and repetitious, so although you need to say it each time, particularly when you are new to objective writing or when you are reviewing your objectives, you only need to write it once, as a blanket opening statement, when you create your list of objectives for your learners.

Basic Rule 15

If your objectives are written for your or someone else's benefit, and not for your learners to use as their learning guide, then the objectives benefit no one.

objective. Avoid writing overly complex objectives that may confuse the learner and undermine the point of the training.

Table 4-3 shows some examples of learning objectives that are simpler than the three-part objectives advocated by Mager. Nevertheless, they are still behavior based and learner centered.

ASTD has published a book in this series, *Training Design Basics* (Carliner, 2003), which can assist you with objective writing. Your responsibility as a trainer now is to understand the parts of a good objective and to ensure that the objectives you write tell the learners exactly which behaviors they are expected to perform. Otherwise, what's the point?

Table 4-3. Examples of some simple, effective learning objectives.

Here are some examples of well written objectives that were created for a training program on instructional design:

At the end of this program you will be able to:	
	1. Discuss the advantages and disadvantages of systematic instructional design.
	2. State the purpose of analysis.
	3. Define various types of analysis.
	4. Describe the process and products of a learning needs analysis.
	5. Perform a job/task analysis.
	6. Differentiate between knowledge and performance objectives.
	7. Construct useful, behavior-based learner objectives.

Five Facts About Objectives

The whole subject of objectives can be confusing, but here are five facts that you should keep in mind to be a successful trainer:

1. Base your objectives on a solid training analysis. From analysis, you can determine if your training will bridge a performance gap and help your organization achieve its mission.

2. Objectives tell you if your training is on track. Objectives let your managers know what's going to be covered and can tell you if your analysis is correct. Plus, you can avoid wasting time, money, and effort by keeping your training efforts relevant and focused as you develop course materials. Furthermore, objectives at the program level allow SMEs to make sure a program covers all the right content.

3. Objectives tell the trainers what should be covered in the program. This is especially true if you are not the actual trainer and you are preparing material for someone else. (See Carliner's *Training Design Basics* (2003) for more on preparing course workbooks.) Objectives tell you which points are important and keep training focused.

4. Objectives serve as a roadmap to determine what your learners should get out of the training. If done correctly, you can almost guarantee that your learners will leave your course with the required skill.

5. Objectives are vital to evaluate how well your training worked. Trainers call the assessment of your training success *evaluation*. The evaluation may be a written test or a performance demonstration of a new skill. Measurement and evaluation is a whole field of study, and a few good resources on this subject are listed in the Additional Resources section at the end of this book.

Noted

A training curriculum is a series of training courses that work together to meet a higher level need for training. For example, you may have a six-course training curriculum (also often called a training system) to train an employee to be a bank branch manager or a five-course curriculum to develop good communications skills in all supervisors at your company.

Basic Rule 16

Trainee evaluation that is not based on and directly related to well-defined objectives cannot evaluate what the learner has learned.

Getting It Done

The ability to write learner-centered objectives is absolutely critical to the process of designing training. Through practice and study, you can develop this skill as you continue your development as a trainer. Use tables 4-1, 4-2, and 4-3 to guide you as you construct a few objectives of your own in exercise 4-1.

Exercise 4-1. Practice writing objectives.

Here are some learning objectives. Can you spot what's wrong with them? Rewrite them, being sure that they

- are measurable and observable
- are based on Mager's three elements of objective writing
- contain a behavioral verb.

1. The learner will know the proper way to form a widget.

_____

2. The learner will understand the reasons behind giving good customer service.

_____

3. The learner will be familiar with the safety precautions related to using a 12-gauge shotgun.

_____

4. The learner will perform and document a general radiation survey.

_____

5. The learner will be able to efficiently change a light bulb.

_____

Now, reflect on the role of objectives not only in your training, but also in the larger context of your organization and its mission. Complete exercise 4-2.

Exercise 4-2. Learning objectives revisited.

1. What is used as a basis for writing objectives and why is this important?

2. List five different ways in which trainers use objectives.

_____

_____

_____

_____

_____

3. Make your own behavioral verb list. Think about the particular training that you'll be doing and see if you can list 10 or 15 behavioral verbs that would likely be used in that type of training. Now break your list down into knowledge verbs and performance verbs if you can. If you can't, consider if there are no performances attached to your training or if you just missed them.

4. Try writing some objectives of your own. Be sure to put all three parts of Mager's elements (behavior, criteria, conditions) in each one, and start each with the phrase, "The learner will . . . ." to ensure that it is learner centered, as well. Ask a colleague who knows about objectives to critique yours, and then rewrite them.

You've been introduced to evaluation techniques in this chapter. The next chapter will continue this topic with a look at all of the various forms of evaluation a trainer might be called upon to use.

5

The Basics of Evaluation

What's Inside This Chapter

Here you will see how to:

▶ Determine the level of evaluation you want to do

▶ Decide what to evaluate

▶ Distinguish among the various levels of evaluation and the tools that are used in each.

Evaluation is often called assessment, particularly when evaluating learning that results from training. You may be slightly confused about the term *assessment* showing up in the context of evaluation because the term was used in the earlier discussion of training analysis.

The best advice is to not worry about terms and keep in mind that analysis occurs *before* the training takes place. Evaluation usually is done *after* the training. If "assessment" occurs before the training happens, it is part of the analysis process. If the "assessment" is done after the training, you can call it evaluation.

In the training profession, you will hear about four or five levels of evaluation that can tell you how effective your training has been. Donald Kirkpatrick was the first to specifically identify the four levels of evaluation (table 5-1) in his seminal book *Evaluating Training Programs: The Four Levels* (1994). Since Kirkpatrick's work, a fifth level, which deals with evaluating the outcomes of training in relation to the goals and objectives of the organization, is often discussed in conjunction with Kirkpatrick's four levels. The Additional Resources section of this book lists a number of publications that will give you a bit more background in evaluation.

Table 5-1. Kirkpatrick's (1994) four levels of evaluation.

Level	Name	Description
1	Reaction	Measures the extent to which learners liked the training program (e.g., content, experience, instructor, media).
2	Learning	Measures the extent to which the training improved learners' knowledge, principles, skills, or attitudes. Measures of learning can include paper-and-pencil tests, skill practices, performance checklists, work scenarios, or simulations.
3	Behavior	Measures the extent to which learners applied learned skills or knowledge back on the job.
4	Results	Measures the extent to which the training made a difference to business results. Results can include cost savings, work output improvement, quality changes, or achievement of corporate objectives.

Evaluation can be as complex or as simple as you want to make it. The bottom line about evaluation is to do what makes sense for your training. Perhaps you only want to know whether or not your learners liked the training you provided (level 1 evaluation). If this were the case, you would be wasting your time designing complex

Basic Rule 17

Before you begin any type of evaluation, ask yourself this simple question: "What will I do with this information once I collect it?" If your answer is "I don't know," you still have work to do.

evaluations that would tell you the business results of your training (level 4 evaluation). The following sections provide you some basic information on Kirkpatrick's four levels plus the additional fifth level that others use and how to best use them in your training.

Level 1 Evaluation

Kirkpatrick's level 1 evaluates the learner's opinion of the training. It is usually done as a questionnaire—often called a "smile sheet"—based on a response scale called the Likert scale. You have most likely used this type of scale to rate an organization's customer service representatives or to evaluate types of service or products. A Likert scale offers various responses, oftentimes ranging from "strongly agree" to "strongly disagree."

Once you know that you need to evaluate your training and understand clearly what you intend to do with data once you collect it, your next job is selecting the right evaluation instrument. (By the way, the word *instrument* is another one of those trainer-speak words.) An instrument simply describes the range of methods that you might use to collect data—paper handouts, computer scoring sheets like you used for standardized tests, or an Internet-based instrument.

Many companies use level 1 evaluation for all courses, whereas others are much more selective in their use of level 1, using this approach only for courses that they know will be revised or that they have a particular reason for evaluating. Just remember that when you use level 1 or any of the evaluation techniques mentioned in this chapter, you must be able to justify the specific technique's use. If your learners are confused or even insulted by the type of evaluation you ask them to do, you might lose a powerful asset of your position as trainer—credibility.

Noted

Knowing in advance the purpose of the evaluation will also help you to design the evaluation instrument or even decide on a different method of evaluation than the one you originally planned. It will help you keep superfluous questions out of your questionnaire (if that is the evaluation tool you've selected) and help you to create questions that will give you the data you're after.

Figure 5-1 provides some examples of level 1 evaluation instruments. The first, as you can see, utilizes a Likert scale. You can use these examples as guides when you develop your own instruments later or continue your trainer education.

Level 2 Evaluation

You should consider level 2 if the purpose of your evaluation is to determine how well learners have mastered your training objectives. You will remember that in chapter 4 criterion-referenced instruction, testing, and evaluation were discussed briefly. If you've designed your training in accordance with the learning objectives (criteria), it is a simple matter to design a level 2 evaluation.

Consider this example: The objective, "The learner will be able to list the five functions of a reactor vessel," is criterion referenced to the question, "In the space below list the five functions of a reactor vessel." In contrast, the objective, "The learner will be able to state the four classifications of call signals," is not criterion referenced to the question, "For each of the call signals listed below, write its type in the space provided," because the objective asks for a statement of fact while the question requires recognition of characteristics.

Level 2 evaluation includes instruments such as a traditional paper-and-pencil test or a performance checklist (figure 5-2) or even an observational evaluation that requires the learner to demonstrate that a skill has been mastered.

You should keep in mind that level 2 evaluation instruments are a criterion-referenced "art form" that require you to balance the actual writing of a test question or the creation of a performance checklist with the original learning objective and the knowledge or skills that relate to that objective.

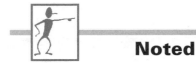

Noted

Performance checklists are also called criterion checklists or performance evaluation instruments, but whatever you call them, they are documents built from a list of performance objectives that are used to evaluate observable performances rather than knowledge during trainee evaluations. An example might be an instruction list that details the 12 steps that must be followed when replacing a battery in a car.

Figure 5-1. Two examples of level 1 evaluation instruments.

For each statement, circle the response that best indicates your opinion:

1. Quality of the material	Poor	Fair	Good	Very Good	Excellent
2. Ability of the facilitator	Poor	Fair	Good	Very Good	Excellent
3. Usefulness of the content	Poor	Fair	Good	Very Good	Excellent
4. Quality of the training facility	Poor	Fair	Good	Very Good	Excellent
5 Relation to your job	Poor	Fair	Good	Very Good	Excellent
6. Quality of the media (slide, video, etc.)	Poor	Fair	Good	Very Good	Excellent
7. Practice sessions	Poor	Fair	Good	Very Good	Excellent
8. Fulfillment of objectives	Poor	Fair	Good	Very Good	Excellent
9. Meeting of your training needs	Poor	Fair	Good	Very Good	Excellent
10. Overall impression	Poor	Fair	Good	Very Good	Excellent

Comments:

Use this scale to indicate your opinion on each of the following:
   3 = agree
   2 = neutral
   1= disagree

1. This course was relevant to what I do on the job. _____
2. I was able to master the course objectives. _____
3. The course was interesting. _____
4. The course gave me practical information. _____
5. The course materials helped me in my learning. _____
6. The role plays were useful activities. _____
7. The trainer helped make the learning easier. _____
8. We had the time to properly complete all the course material. _____
9. The course was well organized. _____
10. Overall the course was worth the time I spent in it. _____

Comments:

Figure 5-2. Example of a performance checklist.

For each of the performances listed below, circle the number that indicates how well the employee performed this task on the job, with a 4 indicating very well, and a 1 meaning not well.

Choose the correct tread size	1	2	3	4
Reverse the interior matrix	1	2	3	4
Lay on the steel belt	1	2	3	4
Sequence the assembly machine	1	2	3	4
Trim excess rubber	1	2	3	4
Inspect for proper seal	1	2	3	4

Other comments concerning learner performance:

Level 3 Evaluation

Level 3 evaluation begins to answer your organization's most pressing question about training: Is the training given being used back on the job? If level 1 is easy, then level 3 begins to really challenge your ability as a trainer. Instead of fairly simple questionnaires, you need to find out if your training has helped with actual job performance. Level 3 evaluations are usually done through a combination of direct observation and questionnaires given to both the learners and their supervisors. These questionnaires may contain general or even specific questions for either supervisors or learners. Here are some examples:

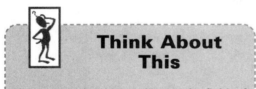

Think About This

Your tests should not be a minefield of trick and difficult questions that your learners have to navigate. Your goal is not to trip up your learners; rather, testing and evaluation are all about learning and, ultimately, performance on the job.

▶ Do you believe your (or the learner's) performance has improved since the training?

> ▶ Which training objective provided you (or the learner) with the most useful information?

> ▶ Describe how you (or the learner) have used the information related to objective 4 on the job.

Many trainers believe that level 3 evaluation should be a standard for every training event, but the truth is that very few level 3 evaluations are done relative to the amount of training given. Why? A simple answer may be the lack of time, support, and money. Both supervisors and employees must take the time to participate in level 3 evaluations, and finding time is a real challenge for most participants.

To do a level 3 evaluation correctly, you must take the time to observe your learners back on the job, talk to supervisors, create questionnaires, and correlate data. In addition, once you have gathered all this data, you must make decisions about how to make training more effective and implement those recommendations.

All these activities add up to a vast amount of time. Some training departments have evaluation specialists who are experts at coming up with such data and making these recommendations. When it comes to level 3 evaluation the reality is that unless you are willing to take on a big job or have someone else who can do it, you should avoid level 3 evaluation.

Level 4 Evaluation

The purpose of a level 4 evaluation, known as either cost-benefit analysis (CBA) or return-on-investment (ROI), is to determine if the benefits that were derived from the training were worth the resources committed to the creation and implementation of your training. As you develop your skills as a trainer, you will hear a good bit about proving the value of training to management.

Determining the costs associated with training is not difficult. You can imagine that you would account for the cost of trainer salary, materials, cost of classroom space, travel costs for the instructor and students, and the cost of lost productivity

Basic Rule 18

Level 3 evaluations offer extremely valuable information about the success of your training. However, do not bother creating evaluation at this level if you do not anticipate having time to implement it.

Think About This

Cost-benefit analysis is often done before a training program is created to decide whether it is worth the time, effort, and money it will take to create it. Return-on-investment evaluation is always done after the training has occurred to decide if the decision to do it was a wise one and if it should be done again. There are many other differences between these two processes, but timing is the main one.

(learners sitting in classes instead of working on the widget line). With the advent of e-learning, your ROI costs might include the cost of computer programs or server rental time.

You might even factor in the costs of not having trained employees as opposed to trained ones and other intangible cost factors, but for now just consider the basics.

Level 5 Evaluation

Level 5 evaluation tells you how well the training relates back to the goals and objectives of your organization. As noted earlier in the discussions of training analysis and objective writing, a consideration of how training relates to the goals and purposes of your company should already be part of your thinking through these two processes. If it wasn't, then level 5 evaluation will probably be very difficult to do as you will be trying to reconstruct decisions that were or were not made before the training began.

Think About This

Doing a full ROI evaluation can be a huge undertaking. Frankly, hardly any trainers do full ROI calculations. ROI is a concept of the moment, but it isn't a reality for most trainers and is certainly outside the scope of this introductory book. The books by Jack Phillips listed in the Additional Resources section provide many useful examples of how to do ROI evaluation.

On the other hand, if you did take your organization's goals and objectives into account during your training needs analysis, then each of your courses and even each of the objectives for those courses should be milestones toward meeting organizational priorities (if your level 2 and 3 evaluations showed that the learners did indeed learn and transfer the learning to the job). Your level 5 evaluation then would simply show the relationship between what was learned and the organization's goals.

Getting It Done

In this chapter, you were introduced to the five levels of training evaluation. You started with the learner's evaluation of the program, traveled through evaluation of the learner, and ended with program evaluation again, but this time in terms of ROI and the goals of the organization. Exercise 5-1 will help you to keep these various evaluation levels straight.

Exercise 5-1. Thinking about evaluation.

1. List Kirkpatrick's four levels of evaluation and what each one measures.

Level	What Does It Measure?
Level 1	
Level 2	
Level 3	
Level 4	

2. List Kirkpatrick's levels again, but this time describe why you would want to use each one. (Hint: If your reason why is the same as what it measures in the previous question, then you've got more thinking to do.)

Level	Why Would *You* Want to Use It?
Level 1	
Level 2	
Level 3	
Level 4	

(continued on page 62)

Exercise 5-1. Thinking about evaluation (continued).

3. Here is a quick case study about an organization with a training need. How can you justify to management the need for doing a level 3 evaluation?

> This organization is a manufacturing company that is having a problem with quality. Analysis determines that it is a training issue as new employees simply do not have the proper techniques for materials handling and manipulation down pat. The training solution is a combination class and laboratory process whereby the learners practice these techniques. Level 2 evaluation shows that they have learned why following these procedures is important and that they can do it in the mock-up lab.

4. Explain the difference between a level 4 evaluation and a level 5 evaluation.

5. Determine which levels of evaluation are used most often in your organization and why. If your answer does not satisfy you, what other levels would you recommend that your organization begins evaluating, and how will you sell management on your evaluation approach?

When you hear the word *trainer,* what comes to mind? The next chapters discuss characteristics that are common to most trainers, though not necessarily all. You'll learn more about the day-to-day activities of a trainer, including what you need to do to actually create a training program, the topic of chapter 6.

6

Creating a
Training Program

What's Inside This Chapter

Here you will see how to:

▶ Utilize a training plan

▶ Decide on a training delivery system that best meets the needs of your organization and your learners

▶ Differentiate among the basic types of training programs

▶ Compare the specific aspects of each type of training program

▶ Decide if and how to use e-learning.

What do most trainers really do? Most trainers create training programs. *Creating,* in this case, includes both developing the program and implementing it. The foundational aspects of program development, such as analysis, objective writing, and evaluation, have already been discussed, but what about the rest of the process?

Like most activities, nothing goes exactly according to plan no matter what your diagram or project plan says. As a trainer, this is something you will have to learn to accept as you get more confident with each activity in the training process, from writing objectives to evaluating your program's success.

You'll also have to get used to the hectic "who's on first" nature of the business. For example, you might end up doing a class needs analysis after a class is already planned because you inherited the project without this work done up front. You might even be required to use your company's new e-learning system, which presents its own set of problems. As a trainer you must relax and figure out the best solution to meet the learning needs of your audience.

Training Plans

Despite the seeming chaos of the job, every training assignment must begin with some type of training plan. This rule holds true whether you are creating a single course or a corporate-wide training program. All training plans have the same components, but they can be more or less complex depending on their purpose. Minimum components of the training plan include training objectives, the intended audience, and a delivery method.

When you create a training plan, it will probably look something like figure 6-1 or 6-2. The first example is a simple plan that you might be able to create with the knowledge you already have. The second example would probably require more experience.

If you compare the two training plan models you will notice similarities and differences. Both training plans require you to state your training objectives, audience, and delivery method. However, the simple plan requires you to account for the cost to develop and deliver the training. This aspect isn't found in the more complex plan as there would usually be supporting documentation in the form of a CBA attached to it. Tracking training costs is a good idea for several reasons. First,

Basic Rule 19

Following a systematic approach to training is important, but there are times when the trainer must go with the flow. In the end, training is about results, not just process.

Figure 6-1. Template for a compact training plan.

1. This course is needed because:

2. The learners will be:

3. The course objectives are:

   a. At the end of this course the learners will be able to:

   b. At the end of this course the learners will be able to:

   c. At the end of this course the learners will be able to:

4. The course will cost $_____ to develop and $_____ to deliver.

5. The design and implementation staff will include these people:

6. The course will be delivered using this method:

your organization will probably ask you for this information, but if you plan to do any type of marketing for your program or plan on looking at the business results from your training (remember level 4 evaluation), cost tracking is essential.

Because this book is targeted mainly toward classroom training, the common question in both plans is accounting of who will do the work, especially if your planning involves any e-learning. You could end up listing e-learning designers and developers as well as several traditional trainers. (See the Additional Resources section for more on e-learning including ASTD's book series on every aspect of e-learning.)

Figure 6-2. Template for a complex training plan.

1. Scope of project (focus)
   Goal
   Audience
   Design time and milestones

2. Delivery
   Content
   Method
   Training time
   Problems and opportunities

3. Objectives

4. Materials

5. Who is involved?

6. Topical outline

7. Administration and evaluation

8. Links

The Delivery Decision

One of the key aspects of your plan is how you intend to deliver your training to your learners. This decision may be simple if your organization delivers 98 percent of its training through a classroom. If your organization has other training delivery options, such as e-learning or self-directed learning, the job gets a little more complex. Your organization may also encourage OJT, mentoring, or coaching as part of the training process, and you will have to account for these company differences in your plan.

No matter how you decide to deliver your training, remember to use common sense and make the best choice for your learners. If e-learning is the best delivery method, use it. However, you should play the devil's advocate when considering e-learning. If, for example, your learners do not have access to fast computers, even the best e-learning can fail.

Noted

Learner guide seems to be the most common term used for learner materials in a classroom setting. The term workbook was once more popular but has picked up a less than desirable connotation and is often equated with a self-instructional or semi-self-instructional package consisting mostly of questions and other assessment activities. Learner manuals usually refer to a policy and procedures manual or the learner's version of a print-based, self-directed learning program. Another term that is commonly used is participant package. Whatever you call them, these documents are an integral part of a classroom process. Oftentimes, they are organized in a three-ring binder usually containing objectives, activities, and readings that are either used in the class or as supplements to the class content.

You can find many models (both in book form and software) that will help you make a training delivery decision. The Additional Resources section lists several such resources. Table 6-1 can help you decide which delivery process might work best for you.

Types of Training Programs

Trainers create four types of training:

- classroom
- one-to-one
- self-directed
- e-learning.

Basic Rule 20

Deliver your training using a method that makes the most sense for your learners and, more importantly, make this decision before you begin creating your training.

Table 6-1. Training delivery processes.

Training Method	Usefulness for Knowledge-Based Material	Usefulness for Performance-Based Material	Usefulness for Changing Attitudes	Usefulness for Developing Interpersonal Skills
Classroom	✪✪✪	✪	✪✪✪✪	✪✪✪✪
On-the-Job Training	✪✪	✪✪✪✪	✪	
Self-Directed Learning	✪✪✪✪	✪	✪	✪
E-Learning	✪✪✪✪	✪✪	✪✪	✪

E-learning is the wildcard in the list. It is oftentimes used in conjunction with one of the first three delivery methods. The result is called *blended learning*.

Classroom Programs

Despite the growth of e-learning and alternative training delivery methods, the classroom remains the most pervasive training method. In fact, a recent ASTD *State of the Industry Report* noted that more than 70 percent of all training is still conducted in classrooms. E-learning accounted for only 8.8 percent of training, and 7 to 9 percent of training was attributed to the on-the-job category (Van Buren & Erskine, 2002).

Noted

Blended learning is as simple a concept as its name suggests. It is the blending of two or more types of training into one program. The first blended learning was a combination of e-learning prework followed by a classroom, but today it might mean any combination of different training types or a number of subtypes.

The reason for the classroom emphasis is simple—a classroom is still the most effective way to train. E-learning is the best solution in many cases (training a worldwide salesforce on a new product for example), but for teaching knowledge and skills, classrooms are still king.

The following sections address the two major elements of classroom training: the lesson plan and learner materials.

The Lesson Plan. As a trainer, you need to be familiar with two types of lesson plans:

- those you create to use in a class you will teach
- th ou create for other trainers (also called facilitators) to use in classes th

A could be pretty minimal if you are very famil consist of just a set of training for someone else
m erial will be
c

ctions ("Show
you create for
s. A good facil-
plan and, with a

in a classroom. Trainers
uch as meeting facilitator,
ic trainer functions. A sep-
n *Basics* will be published in

tator team depends on both
nowledge of the content and a
created by the trainer and used
upporting learner materials must
be ad

Figures 6-5 a for lesson plans that will help you
understand the concept.

Noted

Classroom media are things like flipcharts, models, drawings, overhead projections, or PowerPoint presentations. A good lesson plan delineates what media should be used when and may even include drawings of the media. The plan may or may not discuss how the media should be used effectively, depending on the experience of the facilitators who will be using it.

Learner Materials. You'll note that the lesson plan templates in figures 6-3 and 6-4 call for the learners to complete various activities, view Microsoft PowerPoint slides, and discuss the points made. The lesson plans also call for other activities and techniques to engage the learners such as small group interactions and in-class readings.

These aspects of being a trainer are part of the process of instructional design, which is covered in the companion book in this series, *Training Design Basics*. For now, just note that this material must be created and incorporated into your lesson plan. The most important point to remember whether you arecreating lesson plans or designing an activity to encourage learning is that all training should be learner centered. You, as the trainer, are there to make sure that the focus is in the right place.

As previously noted, this book doesn't tell you how to develop the activities and other materials that your lesson plan describes. However, you should be aware of the basic elements of a learner package and the purpose behind each of those elements. A learner package is a printed document that contains a basic outline of your course and its objectives. The package contains such items as directions for learner-based activities, supplemental readings, and perhaps a list of information resources.

Think About This

Lesson plans, instructor guides, or facilitator materials all have the same purpose. These materials help a classroom trainer to train. Lesson plans are most often found in a detailed outline format. A good lesson plan tells a classroom trainer everything needed to conduct a class successfully. Instructor guides often include long narratives that explain how to run an activity, debrief a role play, or use a graphic effectively. You should always include more detailed information if the trainer delivering the information is not familiar with the subject being taught.

Figure 6-3. Excerpt from lesson plan created in two-column format.

Lesson Plan # 334
Program Title: Basic Training
Time: 2 hours
Revision # 00
*Number of Pages: 32**

Content Outline	Activities and Media

Objective: Differentiate between an audience analysis and other analysis forms
 	
III. Audience Analysis
  A. What is an audience analysis?
  B. When do we want to do one?
	
	• Have the learners read pages 23 and 24.
	• Show slide 12 and ask the question out loud.
	• After discussion, show slide 13 and discuss.

C. What are the best techniques?	• Break learners into small groups and have them try an audience analysis with each group using a different technique. • Using slide 14, discuss their success.
D. What should the product of our audience analysis be?	• Discuss their conclusions from the SGI. • Use slide 15 to wrap up discussion of products.

* Note that only one page of the lesson plan is shown here.

This section will discuss

▶ classroom media
▶ on-the-job training
▶ job aids
▶ mentoring
▶ coaching.

Basic Rule 21

To ensure consistency in training, all your classroom programs must include both a lesson plan for use by the instructor and learner materials that will help the learner learn.

Figure 6-4. Excerpt from a lesson plan created in four-column format.

Lesson Plan # 334
Program Title: Basic Training
Time: 2 hours
Revision # 00
Number of Pages: 32*

Objective	Content Outline	Activities and Media	Time
Objective: Differentiate between an audience analysis and other analysis forms	III. Audience analysis A. What is an audience analysis? B. When do we want to do one?	• Have the learners read pages 23 and 24. • Show slide 12 and ask the question out loud. • After discussion, show slide 13 and discuss.	15 minutes
	C. What are the best techniques?	• Break trainees into small groups and have them try an audience analysis with each group using a different technique. • Using slide 14, discuss their success.	20 minutes
	D. What should our analysis products be?	• Discuss their conclusions from the SGI. • Use slide 15 to wrap up discussion of products.	10 minutes

* Note that only one page of the lesson plan is shown here.

Table 6-2 consists of a checklist you can use to help you select some items you might want to add to your learner package.

Table 6-2. Learner package checklist.

Some Items for Learner Packages
☐ Learning objectives
☐ An introduction to the training
☐ Any reading materials learners will need in class or after
☐ Instruments or surveys the learners will take
☐ Worksheets for skill practices
☐ Role-play instructions
☐ Case studies and associated questions or worksheets
☐ Feedback forms
☐ Special directions for in-class activities
☐ Any instructions or other materials for games or simulations that will be done in class
☐ Job aids
☐ Self-evaluations or quizzes
☐ References, bibliographies, or suggested reading lists
☐ Glossary
☐ Class evaluations

Think About This

What is the purpose of the learner package? The learner package extends the classroom training process into the orbit of the learner. It is a printed document that contains at least a basic outline of the course and the course objectives. Other items you may include are directions for learner-based activities (such as games, role plays, or case studies); places to take notes; listings of books, magazines, and Websites for further information on various topics; and even entire supplemental readings. Once again, the most important aspects (beyond the objectives) are the activity directions, summaries, and so forth. If you find you have no need for a learner package for your classroom because you don't have any of the things listed here, you need to go back and revise your lesson plan. Something very important is missing!

Classroom Media

Media can be defined as "whatever transmits instruction" (ASTD, 2000). Classroom media can include flipcharts, overheads, PowerPoint slides, videos, models, and other learning tools that will help your learners. Every trainer must understand and know how to select appropriate media. Among the choices you must consider are these (ASTD, 2000):

- ▶ learner materials
- ▶ video, audio, transparencies, slides (photographic or PowerPoint), flipcharts, whiteboards, blackboards
- ▶ interactive video, CBT programs, Internet, intranet, or other computer multimedia
- ▶ recorders, computers, projectors, cameras, simulators.

One-on-One Training

As noted in chapter 1, training probably began with one master teaching one student how to accomplish some task. This section will discuss several types of one-to-one training including OJT, job aids, mentoring, and coaching.

On-the-Job Training

As you might expect, OJT happens on the job site and not in the classroom. The concept is a close cousin to apprenticeship, but it has been studied, refined, and improved. On-the-job training is now much more structured and relies on thorough analysis, well-written objectives, and clear instructions in the trainer's guide and in the learner materials.

Noted

The phrase train the trainer *refers to training in facilitation skills for trainers. This book and the other books in this series are tools for your own train-the-trainer course. Every trainer is constantly upgrading his or her skills and expertise as facilitators or instructional designers. Some trainers develop skills as a performance consultant (chapter 9), or they make the transition to e-learning.*

It's important to remember that fifty masters teaching the same skill are likely to give 50 different sets of instructions, creating more problems than solutions. Consistency is everything. That's why all the processes you use for creating classroom training need to be part of your structured OJT program plan, including evaluation.

Usually the OJT learner evaluation is in the form of performance-based checklists because OJT is most often used for skills-based training, such as widget making in a manufacturing setting. Study figure 6-5 to get an idea of how you might go about creating good OJT as a trainer.

Job Aids

A discussion of job aids (basically "cheat sheets" for your learners) is

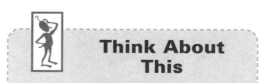

Think About This

Training modules are found most often in self-directed learning programs, but classes are also divided into modules. Essentially, modules help you segment your training, and they provide convenient stopping points for your learners.

appropriate here because job aids are very much associated with OJT. Job aids might include correctly filled out forms, worksheets, a procedural list, photos or diagrams, flow charts with associated task lists, detailed schematic drawings, or even Post-It notes with word-processing shortcuts written on them and stuck on a computer monitor!

Job aids reduce training time and support learning. For example, every time you take off in a commercial airplane, the pilots use a job aid (a checklist, in this case) to make sure that the proper speed is maintained, wing flaps are properly pitched, and other vital tasks are performed to ensure a safe flight. The key to creating good job aids is to organize the information according to how the user will actually use the information step by step.

Mentoring

Mentoring is a close cousin of OJT. Generally, an experienced person helps a person new or less experienced at a job or process to develop skills. In most instances, this is an unstructured process that's not really training. No objectives or guides are

Basic Rule 22

To develop their training skills, all trainers need evaluation of their classroom skills. Don't be shy about soliciting feedback. Trainers are always learning to be better trainers.

Figure 6-5. A suggested outline for developing OJT.

1. Write objectives

2. Develop materials for both learner and OJT trainer
    A. Provide key learning points to trainer and learner
    B. List expected results
    C. Provide work standards that will be used in the training
    D. Provide a sequence of major activities to be done
    E. Highlight the demonstration(s)
    F. Provide a performance checklist for observation and evaluation

3. Prepare the trainer
    A. Provide information on learners (e.g., background, attitudes, age)
    B. Discuss techniques for training one to one
    C. Provide training model such as this:
        —Tell learner what is to be done
        —Show learner how to do it
        —Supervise learner practice
        —Evaluate learner under normal working conditions
        —Provide follow-up support if needed
    D. Provide information on preparing learner for trainer
        —Describe the purpose of OJT session
        —Explain how the session will be conducted
        —Anticipate problems that may occur
        —Explain how the learner will be evaluated
    E. Discuss keys to an effective demonstration
    F. Discuss observation and evaluation tools

Noted

Here's an idea: Have your learners create their own job aids. Provide learners with a template for a job aid and perhaps a skeleton outline of the most important points. After that, the learners can create a job aid that works just for them.

provided for the mentor, and success is hard to measure except by directly observing some improvement in the mentee's performance.

Some organizations have attempted to structure mentoring by creating training programs for the mentor on how to be a good mentor. Contracts are signed,

Basic Rule 23

If you use on-the-job training, make sure that it is structured to ensure consistency from trainer to trainer and from learner to learner. Evaluation is the only way to know for sure that training is occurring in a consistent fashion.

and evaluation is carried out. Structured mentoring is done on the job and usually includes a very detailed mentoring guide and a learner guide, as well. The mentoring is based on analysis, includes very specific objectives, and involves criterion-referenced evaluation. Some programs even include an apprenticeship period that allows the learner to take over some of the mentor's responsibilities.

As you develop your training skills, mentoring is a good tool to have in your trainer's toolkit. If you use this technique correctly, your organization will have an easy way to create a highly effective training process that gets the learner into the work environment in a hurry. In addition, mentoring sharpens the mentor's own skills. The major difference between mentoring and OJT is that the mentoring process is usually longer and more continuous; it also relies on managers or master performers rather than on specified OJT trainers.

Coaching

The term coaching usually signifies a process that is much less structured than either OJT or mentoring. It is often not training at all, but rather a supervisory process that is used to help correct employee problems or enhance the employee's development. Coaching can also be a process by which an outside agent assists individuals in the same way, either helping them with areas of the job that need improvement or assisting in the development of new skills.

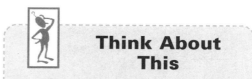

Think About This

Don't make the mistake of using a job aid instead of training. Too often, organizations pass out a procedure manual (basically a series of job aids) and forgo training. This is not a very effective way to help learners. Good trainers use job aids effectively and train learners how to use them.

Basic Rule 24
Use job aids whenever possible to reduce training time and increase learning retention.

Coaching is often prescriptive with no two employees requiring quite the same coaching, or sometimes the same type of coach. Coaching might be considered a training process if new skills are mastered during coaching, Coaching does take a great deal of experience and understanding, so be careful about suggesting this training tool.

Self-Directed Learning
Self-directed learning (SDL), or self-instruction, is often thought of as a training process without a trainer. That is not exactly true. In reality, a trainer is an important a part of SDL and simply plays a different role. If you choose to develop a SDL program, you will still have to go through the traditional process to develop training including analysis, writing objectives, developing test questions, and creating learner materials. More important, SDL must be very precisely created because there is no trainer interaction. Anything you leave out cannot be made up by a live trainer (unless the learner wants to follow up with an email).

Noted

A training tool that's closely related to job aids is a performance support system (PSS). A PSS is basically a complex job aid or series of aids that help the learner do the job or troubleshoot common problems. Policy and procedure manuals are performance support systems as are decision tables and some types of flowcharts. An electronic performance support system (EPSS) is essentially an online PSS. Online wizards for software programs and online help programs are examples of EPSS. A computer program that allows a telephone-based customer service representative to enter customer questions or complaint information and then provides a way or choice of ways for the representative to meet the customer's need is another example of an EPSS.

Noted

A coach is a person who helps another to figure out what he or she should begin to do, continue doing, or do differently. Coaches usually help their clients focus on goals rather than form them. Afterward, they provide feedback on progress made toward the achievement of those goals. Coaching is done usually by supervisors, or it is part of management development. You might be involved in team coaching, personal coaching, or even distance coaching by telephone or email.

Because SDL is a high-wire act, trainers need to ensure that any SDL created is on target. Getting an outside review of an SDL program is essential. This step should include rigorous reviews of your course objectives, and review questions to ensure that they are criterion referenced. Finally, trainers will run a test of the completed program (a beta test) with the target audience group to ensure the program is complete.

Basic Rule 25
Self-directed learning must be precisely created because your learners have no backup live trainer to help.

E-Learning

E-learning is just another way to deliver training. E-learning has been described in a number of ways and called by other names including distance learning, learning technology, CBT, and computer-mediated learning. Marc Rosenberg (2001) offers a useful definition that serves as the basis for discussion in this book: "E-learning uses Internet technologies to deliver a broad array of solutions that enhance knowledge and performance. Its three fundamental criteria are that it runs on a computer network, utilizes a Web-based platform such as a Web browser, and integrates a broader spectrum of solutions than simply training."

E-learning as a practice is the subject of dozens of books. Because this is a book on the basic knowledge that all trainers must possess, the discussion here is limited to the most important points.

Basic Rule 26

Never assume that your learners are automatically self-directed learners. Develop a plan to help them enhance their level of self-directedness.

E-learning is really another way to deliver the three training methods just discussed. In one aspect it allows trainers to hold classes in pretty much the same way as they would in a classroom, except that the classroom is electronic and the learners can be located in front of their own computers all over the world instead of in front of the trainer. These electronic classrooms are termed *synchronous e-learning* because both the learners and the trainer are working together at the same time even if they are in different time zones.

E-learning also has an SDL aspect. The learners call up a program that resides on a server using their desktop computers and complete the program without the assistance of a trainer. This is the process most people envision when they hear the term *e-learning*. Such a program is termed *asynchronous e-learning* because the trainer and learner do not communicate simultaneously. But, that does not mean they don't communicate at all.

Noted

A beta test, which is often termed a design review, is different from a pilot in three major ways. First, the training material need not be in its final format for a beta test. In fact, one of the reasons you do a beta test is to find glitches before you spend all the time necessary to create your final, error-free training materials. Second, the subjects for a beta test are not just members of your target audience as they are in a pilot but should include a SME, another designer, and even a manager or two. This mixture of career levels will provide different points of view, resulting in various takes on the training. Finally, although a pilot is done where the actual training will occur and in the same manner, a beta test may happen anywhere that's convenient, and it may be interrupted or revised on the fly as the trainer deems necessary to get the best review information possible.

Think About This

Self-directed learning programs have become much more sophisticated from the days of correspondence courses, which were the beginnings of SDL programs. The field of SDL has evolved over the years, beginning with programs augmented with slides and videos and leading up to e-learning. Yet, the same rules apply. Trainers still have to develop training programs that stand on their own and are usable by learners at a time and place of their choosing.

Insofar as creating asynchronous programs is concerned, the process is almost exactly the same as other SDL programs. The trainer needs to perform the same strong analysis, create exact objectives, and develop proper criterion-referenced evaluation. The major difference is that the addition of technology means the trainer needs new skills in programming and systems for creating media and activities that the technology can support. This requirement often leads to trainers working in teams with graphic artists and computer programmers to create good asynchronous training programs.

Electronic Bulletin Board

Electronic bulletin boards are Websites where your learners can post their questions, thoughts, and observations concerning the training content. The trainer can discuss these things with them, post his or her own comments and questions, or provide up-to-date information about the class. This is an asynchronous process as the trainer and learners are normally not posting simultaneously, but it can be a part of either synchronous or asynchronous e-learning. It adds a new level of activity to both processes and can be of real value, but it also requires substantial trainer time to monitor, so consider your time constraints before adding a bulletin board to your e-learning program.

Threaded Discussions

Threaded discussions are basically continuing postings to an electronic bulletin board that are focused on a singular topic. They can be started by the trainer or the learners. They last as long as there is someone with something to say on the topic or until the trainer decides it is time to end it. Threaded discussions can add richness to your training program, but they also require your time to guide and monitor them.

Chat Rooms

Chat rooms are similar to bulletin boards, but they are a synchronous process, which means the learners and the trainer are online at the same time. Chat rooms are developing a somewhat shady reputation in general public use, but they are an excellent augmentation to an e-learning program, providing a chance for learners to interact in real time and broaden their discussions on various topics that were brought up in the training. Once again the trainer must be strongly involved in the chat room as a participant, guide, and monitor, so your time availability is a constraint on its use.

Advantages of E-Learning

E-learning can also mean simply an electronic repository where job aids can be stored and downloaded for use, or from which EPSS is accessed. This ability, as well as the use of chat rooms and electronic bulletin boards, makes e-learning a useful delivery system for one-to-one training as well.

As e-learning continues to grow, it continues to add new concepts and requirements to the trainer's basis of knowledge. These include such ideas as reusable learning objects, learning management systems, knowledge management, learning portals, and e-learning as a training strategy.

Online Facilitation Skills

A major mistake that trainers make is to assume that if they have good classroom facilitation skills, these skills will transfer to the computer environment. Synchronous (actual live facilitation online) training requires all the skills of a good classroom trainer and technical skills to make best use of the hardware and software. To be an online facilitator, you must know how to run the computer system your organization has provided, use the software properly, add graphics and video elements, make use of response mechanisms, and be familiar with any number of other aspects that are specific to the software.

Basic Rule 27

Good classroom training skills do not automatically transfer to the computer environment.

Getting It Done

In this chapter you've seen how to create various types of training programs, including classroom, one-to-one, and self-directed formats. Complete exercise 6-1 to sharpen your skills on the basics of developing training programs.

Exercise 6-1. Creating your training plan.

1. Use one of the training plan models provided in this chapter to create a training plan for a program you are working on or plan to work on. Were there any aspects you believe you should have covered that were not part of the model? If so, revise the model so that it becomes your own customized version of a training plan.

2. Think back to classroom-based programs that you attended. List five characteristics that made them good and three things that you think could have been improved. How might this list help you in your utilization of the classroom method?

Characteristics of a Good Program	Things That Could Be Improved
1.	1.
2.	2.
3.	3.
4.	.
5.	

3. Have you ever been a learner in an OJT process? Was it a good or bad experience? If it was good, list the things that made it so. If it was bad, what would you have done differently?

4. Are you a self-directed learner? Utilize an instrument such as the Self-Directed Learning Readiness Scale (www.hrdq.com) or the Learner Autonomy Profile (www.hrdenterprises.com) to assess your readiness for self-directed learning. You might want to check out your learners with these instruments as well.

(continued on page 84)

Exercise 6-1. Creating your training plan (continued).

5. In this chapter you were introduced to several terms related to e-learning. Find and define at least five of them.

E-Learning Term	Definition

Now that you have most of the general basics of training under your belt, jump into the next chapter to get into some of the specific skills and tools you'll need to succeed as a trainer.

7

Skills and Tools
Most Trainers Need

■ ■

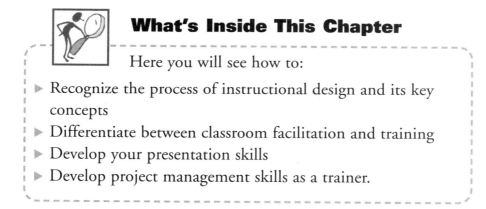

What's Inside This Chapter

Here you will see how to:

▶ Recognize the process of instructional design and its key concepts
▶ Differentiate between classroom facilitation and training
▶ Develop your presentation skills
▶ Develop project management skills as a trainer.

This chapter discusses some of the key skills you'll need to succeed as a trainer. As noted throughout this book, you will gain awareness as well as some basic knowledge. For a complete understanding of instructional design or presentation skills, you will need further development and study.

Instructional Design

Instructional systems design (ISD) is a term that was noted earlier in this book, but every trainer is quite familiar with the principles of this discipline. Many trainers spend the majority of their time creating training programs and often do not facilitate the classes. An instructional designer may also be a specialist in one aspect of instructional deign, creating only e-learning based programs or designing needs analysis or evaluation instruments.

Nevertheless, the basic skills of an instructional designer are still

- ▶ analysis
- ▶ objective writing
- ▶ evaluation
- ▶ training material development.

Good instructional designers are expert at all of these processes, and use them all for each training program they create, whether it is classroom, SDL, OJT, or e-learning. Instructional designers are often effective classroom facilitators as well.

Instructional design requires discipline and some formal training to do it well. The basic treatment of this topic given here will help you understand enough to ask the right questions at least.

The ISD model is broken into five steps: analysis, design, development, implementation, and evaluation (ADDIE, for short). In analysis, the designer uses various techniques to find out what the training needs are, who the audience is, what tasks need to be trained on, and what delivery system should be used.

In the design phase, objectives and content outlines are created that reflect the tasks, skills, and knowledge that were analyzed in the previous phase. In development, the outlines are turned into learner materials such as learner guides and instructor materials, including lesson plans and media. In the implementation phase, the instructor actually facilitates the class, and, in the evaluation phase, aspects such as the learner's learning, transfer to the job, and ROI are evaluated.

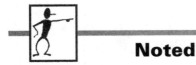

Noted

Some large companies offer training programs to help SMEs or classroom trainers learn instructional design. If your company does not offer this benefit, ISD skills training can be found in college courses and any number of books. Some ISD software exists, but you will still need to know the basics to use the software.

Basic Rule 28

Instructional design is a skill that you can learn.

There is much more to the process, as you can see from some of the books and articles listed in the Additional Resources section.

Classroom Facilitation

Classroom facilitation is a definite skill that all good trainers need, but it is a learned skill. Many SMEs are asked to do classroom training without being equipped with the basic skills; the results can be painful for all concerned. Table 7-1 lists some of the competencies that an effective facilitator possesses.

Classroom facilitation is both a science and an art. Facilitation demands good training materials, but it also requires the facilitator to have a working knowledge of the learners and the basics of learning that have been the subject of this book. A companion book in this series *Facilitation Basics* will be published in the spring of 2004.

Table 7-1. Competencies of a good facilitator.

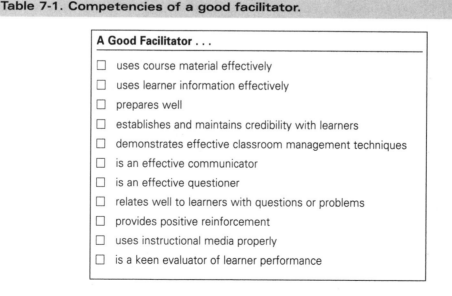

A Good Facilitator . . .

- ☐ uses course material effectively
- ☐ uses learner information effectively
- ☐ prepares well
- ☐ establishes and maintains credibility with learners
- ☐ demonstrates effective classroom management techniques
- ☐ is an effective communicator
- ☐ is an effective questioner
- ☐ relates well to learners with questions or problems
- ☐ provides positive reinforcement
- ☐ uses instructional media properly
- ☐ is a keen evaluator of learner performance

Basic Rule 29
Facilitation is both an art and science. It requires great classroom materials and experience in the process of learning.

Trainers must always keep in mind that the purpose of a classroom facilitator is to help learners acquire the knowledge and skills they need to perform on the job. Keep your training learner centered, and you can't go far wrong.

Presentation Skills

Interestingly, many people (actually a majority) don't like the idea of getting in front of a group at all. In fact, fear of speaking in front of a group is always among the top five fears that people have, right up there with the fear of death and snakes.

To master the trainer skill of presenting, you need to be comfortable speaking in front of people for the purpose of helping them learn. You also need to understand how people learn and how you, as a trainer, can help them in this endeavor. You need well-constructed materials (this goes back to ISD), and you need to know some of the tricks of the trade that help you maintain your learners' interest, provide them with their own individual opportunities to learn (classroom activities), and, at the same time, keep control of the classroom. Table 7-2 lists some of the characteristics of excellent presenters and poor presenters.

You can find many opportunities and courses that can help you hone and practice your presentation skills. Join Toastmasters, or try leading an adult education class or a Sunday school class. If you take a formal approach to learning this skill set, select courses that are short on content and long on practice. They should include discussions of classroom techniques, listening skills, classroom preparation, and classroom control. However, they should also include at least two or three videotaped practice sessions after which you are given time to sit down with the instructor and critique your facilitation. It can be painful to watch yourself, but in the end your learners will love you for doing it.

Unless you have a real need, stay away from classes that seem to teach instructional design skills such as objective writing or evaluation along with facilitation and presentation skills. You should work on those skills in an instructional design program when you are ready for them. Giving you a little bit of everything won't make you much of anything by the end of the program, so choose wisely.

Table 7-2. Characteristics of presenters.

Excellent Presenter Characteristics	Poor Presenter Characteristics
• Reveals passion for subject	• Does not cover objectives promised
• Demonstrates commitment	• Does not allow enough breaks
• Keeps focused	• Has bad nonverbal habits
• Establishes rapport	• Uses habit verbiage (um, like, you know)
• Shows empathy	• Fails to check environment
• Is receptive	• Uses out-of-date material
• Shows confidence	• Does not admit mistakes
• Has integrity	• Uses inappropriate humor
• Maintains credibility	• Acts like an arrogant expert
• Is flexible	• Does not engage the learners
• Has an effective style	
• Demonstrates depth	

For a more comprehensive look at what it takes to be an excellent presenter, see *Presentation Basics* (Rosania, 2003), another book in this series.

PowerPoint Presentations

PowerPoint presentations have become ubiquitous in the training profession and, so, merit a brief discussion here. The software is the default software for nearly all presentations whether used by trainers for classroom programs or organizational meetings. PowerPoint has all but eliminated the use of overhead projectors, which were once a training staple, and has made it possible for every trainer to be a graphic artist.

Here are 10 rules that every trainer needs to know about PowerPoint presentations:

1. Keep the design clean.
2. Don't add too many effects.
3. Keep the background subtle.
4. Use clip art sparingly.
5. Use the right graph style for the data.
6. Limit colors to three per slide.
7. Adhere to the six-by-six format: no more than six words per line and no more than six lines per slide (figures 7-1 and 7-2).

8. Use light colors on dark backgrounds.
9. Keep sound and music clips brief.
10. Always practice your show by projecting it to check for projection quality.

Project Management

Training is not a simple "let's do it" process. It requires time and energy to develop and implement it properly, and project management skills help the trainer control all the processes necessary to move from the feeling that training might be the answer to a performance gap to actually having well-trained and productive employees.

Noted

There are a number of project management systems available, ranging from simple checklists to computer programs that even provide you with reminders when it's time to do something. The best one is the one that works for you.

Every training program needs a project manager to track all the activities that surround the creation and implementation of training. To track the myriad activities that go along with design of a training project, for example, you might use a project plan similar to the one shown in figure 7-3.

Figure 7-1. What's wrong with this PowerPoint slide?

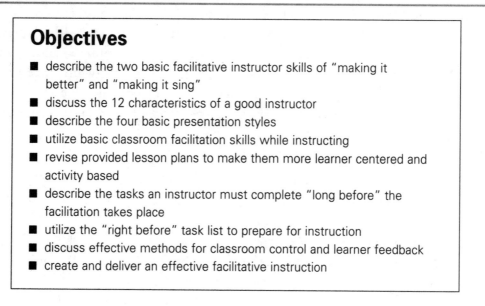

Objectives

■ describe the two basic facilitative instructor skills of "making it better" and "making it sing"
■ discuss the 12 characteristics of a good instructor
■ describe the four basic presentation styles
■ utilize basic classroom facilitation skills while instructing
■ revise provided lesson plans to make them more learner centered and activity based
■ describe the tasks an instructor must complete "long before" the facilitation takes place
■ utilize the "right before" task list to prepare for instruction
■ discuss effective methods for classroom control and learner feedback
■ create and deliver an effective facilitative instruction

Figure 7-2. Adhering to the six-by-six format leads to clean, appealing PowerPoint slides.

Appearance

- **Dress appropriately for the group.**
- **Dress for your comfort.**
- **Don't overpower your message.**
- **Check in the mirror.**

Figure 7-3. Example of a training design project plan.

1. Scope of Project (Focus)
   —Goal
   —Audience
   —Design Time
   —Milestones
2. Objectives of Plan
3. Delivery Plans
   —General Content to Be Delivered
   —Method for Delivery
   —Reason for Training
   —Foreseen Problems
   —Possible Opportunities
4. Material Resources to Be Used
5. Individuals Involved in Project
6. Topical Outline
7. Administration of Project
8. Project Evaluation
9. Links to Other Projects and Processes in Organization

For more information on project management for trainers, check out the Additional Resources section of this book.

Getting It Done

In this chapter you had a brief look at the most important trainer skills—instructional design, facilitation, and project management. Use exercise 7-1 to help you consider your own level of ability related to these skills.

Exercise 7-1. How does ISD relate to what you do?

1. Describe what an instructional designer does.

2. Differentiate between what an instructional designer does and what a classroom facilitator does, and how these differences affect your view of what you do as a trainer.

3. PowerPoint presentations for classroom training are the new standard. What are some of the main problems with the use of PowerPoint presentations?

4. List what you believe are your strengths and areas for improvement as a facilitator based on the lists given to you in the chapter.

So, what's involved in creating a large-scale training program? The next chapter will tell you the basics about how to undertake such a challenge.

8

Training Systems, Marketing, and Maintenance

What's Inside This Chapter

Here you will see how to:

▶ Create a training system
▶ Identify the various types of training systems
▶ Use proven training techniques to create an orientation system
▶ Apply a successful marketing strategy to the training environment
▶ Create an effective training program maintenance strategy.

If you've purchased this book, chances are you are a person who's new to training and looking for the information about what an individual trainer usually does. You may have been asked to actually create or teach a class or course, or—even more daunting—you may have been given responsibility for an entire training program. This chapter will give you a starting point to create a large-scale training program or at least appreciate the responsibility you'd have if you make the transition to full-time trainer.

What Is a Training System?

If you take the time to create a group or family of coursework that will achieve a stated series of training objectives, you've created a training system. For example, a group of SDL modules designed to allow a learner to master a certain set of skills (such as a skill set to be a retail store manager) is a training system. You will notice that this simple example includes the two required components of an individual-level training system: It states a need (high-level training for store managers), and it designates a training method (SDL).

The difference between the training system just for store managers (individual system) and a system that includes all store employees (organization-wide system) would be the addition of another new training component and the designation of an audience. For example, a training system strategy to help individual employees serve customers more efficiently would include an analyzed need, a training method (perhaps some OJT by a more experienced store employee), and designation of a target audience. Note that as you create larger systems the number of components increases.

No matter how you decide to move forward on a training system, just make sure that your decisions are based on well-analyzed organizational training needs and that the system uses training methods that are the most effective and efficient for the organization and the learners.

Development As Training

Another type of training system is a development system. Development differs from training in that in a development system you are preparing learners for new job responsibilities or new positions, not training them to fulfill the tasks of their current

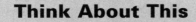

Think About This

Remember that, optimally, training needs analysis is done at different levels in an organization. You begin with the training needs of the whole organization and work down to the individual level. Your training system, or training strategy, will likely parallel your needs analysis in that it will consist of an organization-wide system and individual-level system (or systems) and continue down to the class level where it deals with singular jobs or even tasks.

Basic Rule 30
Your training system should be based on your organization's analyzed needs.

position. Development under this scenario might use the same series of training programs used year after year to develop employees for certain jobs in an organization. Management development programs are good examples of development training strategies, and they are an integral part of HR succession planning systems.

Succession Planning Systems

A succession planning system is used to build what is termed *bench strength* in an organization. In a perfect world a succession planning system would ensure that each position has two or three people ready to move up into it if the need arises and that every employee would be able to move into two or three different positions if required. In these days of reduced staffing and doing more with less, these systems are not as prevalent as they once were. Nevertheless, their underlying concept of developing employees to be ready to move on is still a key issue for trainers.

Individualized Development Systems

A development system for individual employees is a common approach used in most training programs, and, in general, these programs are very prescriptive. They involve a good deal of personal analysis to determine an employee's developmental

Noted

Some organizations deliver the majority of their training through e-learning, making e-learning a high-level (organization-wide) training system. Although this might make the delivery question easier for the trainer, it does make it difficult to find ways to fit all training into one delivery method. That's why most organizations blend e-learning with classroom training.

goals, as well as his or her strengths and areas for improvement. Managers in these systems need skills to help their employees analyze their goals and trainers who partner with managers to help employees find appropriate developmental goals.

If you happened to be a trainer in this situation you would have reduced instructional designer or facilitator roles. Instead, you would be a repository of information on available training resources or at least a guide to such repositories. Trainers in this situation may also counsel both managers and employees as they work toward the creation of individualized development plans such as the one shown in figure 8-1.

Employee Orientation Systems

Employee orientation was once a program that sat firmly in the HR corner of an organization and not really considered part of a training system. However, companies are moving to an orientation system, which includes general orientation and specific orientation for a department, business group, or team. The trainer is often asked to help create these specific, second-level orientations. These second-level systems may involve the use of a number of training methods depending on the environment and resources of the department, group, or team.

Marketing Strategy

A good trainer must also be a good marketer. After all, what good is a great training program that isn't well attended? Trainers often lament this attendance problem and are perplexed with low attendance numbers when good analysis told them that the need for training was clear. Trainers also need to be good marketers of their training decisions, for example, the decision to use a certain delivery method such as e-learning or the decision to use classroom training instead of self-directed learning.

Noted

E-learning has great potential for creating self-directed orientation. For example, organizations now routinely use a company's intranet (an internal, closed-system Internet) to guide new employees through the orientation process. E-learning allows employees to access department and workgroup orientation information and customize their own training.

As a trainer you will quickly learn that getting management support for your decisions is critical to your success as a trainer. The following sections can give you some guidance on marketing to individual employees and your organization as a whole.

Figure 8-1. Example of an individualized development plan.

Learner _____ Date Begun _____

Manager _____ Date Completed _____

Topic _____

Organizational Goal This Learning Will Help Achieve	Personal Goal This Learning Will Help Achieve	Learning Objectives (What the Learner Will Know or Be Able to Do)	Learning Process (Steps Necessary to Achieve the Objectives)	Learning Resources (What Trainers Need to Provide or Help Learners Access)	Target Dates	Evaluation and Transfer of Skills/Knowledge to Workplace

Manager's Signature _____

Learner's Signature _____

Marketing to Individuals

Getting your target audience to attend your training programs is always a challenge for trainers, but many ways exist to help you accomplish this task. This section will give you some basic ideas. Oberstein and Alleman (2003) offer more ideas in their book *Beyond Free Coffee and Donuts: Marketing Training and Development Programs.*

The most important marketing aspect is to make sure that the programs you develop are based on needs of the organization. If you have done this, getting people to attend your sessions is much easier.

You also need to publicize your courses through a newsletter, bulletin board announcements, or in this electronic age, emails.

Word of mouth is still the best advertising, however, and nothing will draw learners to your courses like the common knowledge that they are worthwhile, spread by participants who have already attended.

You might have a learning day at which you introduce your courses by posters in the cafeteria or in a special learning room where employees can see five-minute segments of various courses. This approach also works well if you have a learning lab.

Paper-Based Marketing. Despite the pervasive presence of computers, sometimes a colorful sheet of paper and a copy machine can be your best marketing tools. You can create flyers to insert in paycheck envelopes, post on bulletin boards, deliver through internal mail, and don't forget the good old booklet of course offerings. It's not fancy but it provides a good reference for employees and supervisors who are

Think About This

Lunch-and-learn programs, also called brown bag training, is a process of providing small training programs at lunchtime to employees who are interested in continuing their learning. The topics are very focused, and the method might be a presentation, discussion, or even a video. These processes are also great marketing tools for the trainer as they show what the training department can do, and provide a ready-made forum for announcing new training initiatives that are on the way.

looking for a learning intervention. You might create a periodic learning newsletter that is delivered through inter-office mail or a column in your organizational newsletter.

Electronic Marketing. You can really wow your learners using the computer that most of your learners work at all day long. Here are a few ways to effectively market through electronic means:

- ▶ electronic flyers that pop up on internal computers from time to time
- ▶ email announcements of new courses
- ▶ announcements on the company's home page of new offerings
- ▶ an internal Webpage of learning offerings that not only explains what they are but provides a link to them if they are electronic
- ▶ special bulletins that come out whenever something different happens in learning
- ▶ an electronic news page that is published periodically to bring learners up to date on learning processes.

Marketing to Management

Once trainers have created a training strategy, it is often little more than sheets of paper without management support. You need to garner support for your projects from management through a marketing strategy.

Again, the best marketing technique is to have courses that meet organizational needs. Everything else in marketing rests on this foundation. Here are a few additional tips:

- ▶ To gather management support, create executive summaries of your courses that managers can sit through in 15 or 20 minutes.
- ▶ Go to management meetings at all levels, and discuss with the managers how your courses meet their needs.
- ▶ Hold individual meetings with managers and supervisors to show them the objectives and topic outlines, and then ask for their support.
- ▶ Ask that announcements of new training programs be a part of every management meeting and then write those announcements for the meeting chairs.

▶ If your company has a management orientation, ask for time or space there to discuss training and your programs.

▶ If you do not have a management orientation, ask HR for a list of new managers and visit them during their first few days.

▶ Distribute giveaways, such as pens, notepads, or mouse pads, on which your name and telephone number are imprinted so the managers can call if they have a training problem.

Basic Rule 31

Trainers need to know how to market to both their learners and to management.

Maintenance Strategy

So, once you've planned, created, and deployed your training, it's time to sit back and relax, right? Wrong. You need to keep your information up to date so that it's accurate when it's used again. Training maintenance is especially important if you worked with an SME to create a training course for others in your organization, and it's absolutely critical for training on rapidly evolving topics, such as information technology.

The best way to create a maintenance strategy is to devise a system that requires each training program to be reviewed at regular intervals. Depending on the program and its content, this review might happen every six months, every year, or even every two years.

The review examines key content to determine if it needs to be changed, added to, or deleted based on the needs of your learners. A trainer might make these decisions based on an evaluation of the effectiveness of the class. Good trainers often create their own systems that track when courses were launched, when they were last reviewed, and what changes are needed. You should make maintenance a priority and take this responsibility seriously.

Basic Rule 32

All trainers need to keep track of the training they produce. Create a system to track your training and keep your work current.

Getting It Done

In this chapter you were introduced to additional general trainer tasks such as how to create training systems and how to market and maintain them. Use exercise 8-1 to help you practice these processes.

Exercise 8-1. Thinking about training systems in your organization.

1. Analyze your own organization to find out what training systems exist. Are they based on good training needs analysis? Do they work? What delivery methods do they use? What changes would you make to make them more effective or efficient?

2. Does your company have any development systems? If so, compare them to your training systems to understand the purpose and procedures of each a little better. Do they use different delivery methods? If so, why do you think each delivery method was chosen, and if you don't think it was the right choice, what would have been better? Why?

3. Design an e-learning-based orientation system (at least on paper) for your organization. What content should be created to reside on your e-learning Webpage? What links need to be added to send the trainee to other Websites? Once there, how will you guide them to the right information on these sites? What else will need to be created to make the most effective e-learning orientation for your learners? What arguments will you use to get your concept approved by management?

(continued on page 102)

Exercise 8-1. Thinking about training systems in your organization (continued).

4. Does there seem to be a marketing strategy for training in your organization? If so, what is it? Does it seem to be effective as gauged by attendance and interest? If not, how would you market training to your organization?

5. Create a maintenance strategy for any training program that you are responsible for. How did you decide upon the frequency of reviews? What will you consider in each review and why? How will you find the time to do any necessary revisions?

So far in this book you've looked at the very basic aspects of being a trainer, but there is much more to training than what's been covered here. The last chapter will look at some more specialized training concepts and give you a brief explanation of them.

9

The Universe
of the Trainer

■■■■■■■■■■■■■■■■■■■■■■■■■■■■■■■■■■■■■■

 What's Inside This Chapter

Here you will see how to:

▶ Explore the myriad ways that trainers can help organizations
meet business goals and individuals perform better in their
work lives—and, perhaps, their lives outside the workplace
▶ Integrate additional training concepts into your trainer-
speak vocabulary
▶ Find a training niche that will meet your personal and
career goals.

Where Do You Fit in the Universe of Training?

This book has introduced you to the basics of training, but how can you apply this
newfound knowledge? What can you as a trainer do to help your organization and
the individuals that comprise it meet their goals?

As you delve deeper into the field of training, you'll see that there are volumes
of books and articles devoted to the topic. The rest of this chapter introduces you to

just a few of the options that might be available to you as a trainer. At the very least, the concepts introduced here will expand your trainer-speak vocabulary. The concepts discussed are somewhat advanced and each would require at least one book—if not an entire graduate course—to cover it adequately. They are presented here simply to help familiarize you with the terms and their underlying concepts, so that if you feel you need to learn more, you'll at least have a head start.

Human Performance Improvement

Human performance improvement (HPI), sometimes called human performance technology (HPT) or simply performance technology (PT), is a term you will surely hear as you develop your training skills. Whatever you call it, the work and the principles are the same and are, in many ways, based on common sense.

The idea behind HPI is that training cannot answer every performance problem in the workplace. Sometimes other solutions, often called *interventions,* are the answer. For example, if a company's customer service representatives are slow to process orders, training won't help if the computer system is inadequate for the job.

HPI professionals are strong proponents of analysis. However, HPI analysis, termed *performance analysis,* looks specifically at performance needs of the organization. Sometimes, but not always, training is the intervention needed to fill the performance needs (called *performance gaps*) of the organization.

The main work of an HPI professional is to find ways to bridge performance gaps using cause analysis to understand the reasons for the gap. As noted earlier, the intervention for closing the performance gap might be training, but in many cases

Noted

A performance gap is the difference between the current performance and the expected performance of some part of the organization. The gap might exist at the organization level (such as an inability to achieve an organizational goal), at a department level (such as not meeting profit projections), or at the level of individuals or work groups (such as not manufacturing enough of a certain component to meet company demand). A gap analysis is done by performance technologists who determine what the desired performance is, what the current performance is, and the extent of the gap between desired and current performance.

training is just a part of a solution. Once the correct interventions are developed and implemented, the HPI process includes evaluation to determine how well the intervention worked. Figure 9-1 is a simplified model of how HPI works.

HPI professionals also can look for opportunities to increase performance in organizations when no apparent gaps exist so that HPI professionals participate in the overall bottom-line strategy of the organization. Among these opportunities might be ways for the organization to gain a further competitive advantage or, perhaps, to augment customer service. After the opportunities are analyzed the process of choosing the proper intervention, creating it, implementing it, and evaluating it are much the same as they are for a performance gap.

Organization Development

Organization development (OD) is a process of planned, systematic organizational change based on the theories of behavioral science. The change occurs

Figure 9-1. A model of HPI

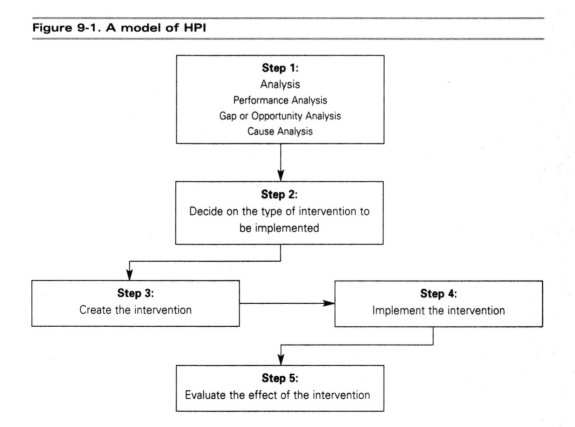

organization-wide, and its purpose is to increase organizational effectiveness and alignment with the organization's stated goals and mission statement. As you might guess, the growth of HPI has supplanted some of the work done by OD professionals, but the profession is still an important part of the organizational life of many companies.

Organization development includes complex concepts that go well beyond the scope of this book, but you should be aware of the basic job of an OD professional. OD practitioners often see themselves as strategic consultants and agents of change who facilitate groups, build teams, and resolve conflicts. Because of the emphasis on the organization as a whole, OD is most often related directly to the executive level of an organization. OD is often a key player in moving forward major changes in an organization such as keeping an organization on track during a major restructuring or reorganization effort.

Change Management

Change management is the process of helping an organization achieve large- or even small-scale change. It includes both training processes and coaching processes. HPI practitioners would say that change management is a subset of their discipline, which is mostly true. It is also a critical aspect of OD.

Change management is a systematic approach to change in which a formal change plan is created and implemented. This plan may include some or all of the following:

- ► a change agenda that's distributed throughout the organization to articulate clearly what the change is, why it's needed, and who is affected
- ► discussions with senior leadership to explain the need for the change and obtain their commitment, support, and personal involvement
- ► workshops for everyone affected by the change to explain its purpose and develop a sense of urgency and commitment
- ► training for workshop facilitators and change leaders to go over in detail the specific aspects of the change itself and the change process as well, so that they can act as change resources
- ► feedback mechanisms to monitor the success of the change process and provide data for midcourse corrections if needed
- ► ongoing reinforcement to keep the process on schedule and maintain the momentum that was engendered by the workshops
- ► an evaluation to determine the success of the change and the change process.

Change management is not simply checking to make sure that all parties have implemented the change. It is a very detailed process that you can use to ensure that the change you are responsible for gets off to a good start and has a better-than-average chance of being accepted by the organization.

Competencies

Competencies are easy to understand but hard to define. They are usually seen as the key performances of master performers. These performances are broken down into the skills and knowledge that comprise them, and then these are regrouped as competencies. The competencies now become performance criteria for all employees who hold the same position as the master performer. Competencies can even be regrouped at higher levels to create broad competency statements for the entire organization.

The problem is that these regroupings can be very different for different organizations and even within an organization. Competencies, therefore, have no generally accepted definitions. For example, one company's competencies might include leadership, interpersonal communications, influencing for results, and relationship building. In another system they might be termed initiative, self-discipline, and empathy. Yet, even with such imprecise concepts, trainers and other HR professionals have created competency models, competency-based training, competency-based recruitment, even competency-based pay.

The best thing to do if your organization is "into" competencies is to forget about the books and magazine articles and first learn what your organization's idea of competencies is. Then, use the resources that most closely match your company's definition to learn what you can. Otherwise, it will be a long, hard, frustrating road to become competent in competencies!

Learning Organizations

The concept of a learning organization is based on a few main concepts including these:

- the idea that employees never stop learning (a process sometimes called continuous learning)
- a belief that employees need to know how to learn so that they can practice continuous learning
- a commitment to the idea that employees must share their learning with everyone in the organization.

The notion of a learning organization is often associated with high-tech industries in which basic knowledge grows and changes very rapidly. Sharing information and learning within the organization is central to continued business success for these organizations.

For example, if a workgroup in a company learns how to solve a particular problem that a customer has had with its product, the group should be able to share with the rest of the organization both the solution and the process it went through to find it. In this way, if another workgroup has a similar problem, it won't have to start from scratch to solve it.

Knowledge Management

Knowledge management attempts to answer the following questions:

- How can the organization minimize time and resources wasted by employees having to relearn things that are already known?
- How can employees' knowledge be captured and made available to everyone in the organization?

Although knowledge management has been popularized recently, it is not a new concept. Computer technology, however, is making the dream of efficiently sharing information a reality. Some organizations have committed significant resources to the idea of collecting, cataloging, and storing vast amounts of data and attempting to ensure that all have access to this information. Some organizations have had success using these complex systems, but getting an entire organization to support and use such a system has proven the most difficult challenge.

Today, much of the knowledge management field is computerized; software programs and even entire systems have been created to collect, catalog, and store the knowledge of the learning organization in vast databases. Unfortunately, organizations that have implemented knowledge management systems still face the problem of getting people to take the time to provide input for the system and to remember to search for the knowledge when they need it.

Internal Consulting

Sometimes organizations will bring in trainers or HPI practitioners as external consultants to conduct training needs analysis, design or develop training programs, or even to carry out the training itself. There is another option, though: Someone from

Noted

Internals need to market their skills to the organization. Because they are already part of the organization and have access to the organization's communications tools such as email, voice-mail, interoffice mail, corporate bulletin boards, meetings, and so forth, marketing is generally easier for internals than it is for external consultants.

within the organization—an internal consultant—can provide the expertise to solve an organizational problem.

An internal consultant's role in an organization is to be available to add his or her know-how to solve a problem or deal with a situation whenever asked. Internal consultants are basically a resource to the organization in their specialty area or areas (much like an external consultant), but organizations often can derive significant savings by tapping their existing internal resources. Internal consultants (sometimes called just "internals") can provide an independent voice for asking the hard questions and providing needed solutions for problems.

A trainer may be an internal consultant for one specific function, such as analysis, or for an entire process, especially if that trainer has made the transition to the role of an HPI professional. Trainers often play the role of internal consultant when they are asked to evaluate a training program the organization is considering purchasing or to advise an organization on developing e-learning or creating a mentoring program. Trainers may also act as internal consultants to individuals working on individual development plans or to the HR department as it develops new-employee orientation packages.

Blended Learning

Blended learning is a concept that is often heard these days, largely as a result of the growth of e-learning. Essentially, blended learning is defined as the combining of two or more training techniques to create a new training design that uses the advantages of each where they do the most good for the learners.

Trainers often use blended learning solutions to prepare learners for classroom training or to break up segments of e-learning. For example, if you are conducting a leadership development class, you might require those who attend take some type

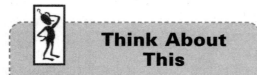

Think About This

Blended learning existed long before there were computers. Your college chemistry class where you spent time in the lecture hall and time in the laboratory was blended learning. Training programs that combine classroom work with OJT are also blends.

of Web-based or computer-based assessment that would gauge leadership potential. The learners would bring the results to class, and these results would be blended with the classroom work. Another example would be a training process that blends mentoring with synchronous e-learning and classroom training.

Also remember, though, that when most people talk about blended learning they will mean a combination of classroom and pre-work, usually as either a computer-based program or an asynchronous e-learning program. It will help you if you find out what they mean by blended learning at the start.

Technology-Based Training

Technology-based training (TBT) has been defined as training in which at least one component of the delivery system plugs in, though recently it has been focused more on training that uses a computer as part of the delivery process. E-learning, CBT, CD-ROM training, Web-based learning, and even video-based training are all TBT in one form or another. Once upon a time, though, even slide shows and filmstrips were considered to be TBT.

The problem is that the boundaries for TBT delivery tend to blur as new technologies are added and as programs become more blended. For example, if you create a training program that is downloaded over your company's intranet to the hard drives of individual computers, and then accessed by the learner from the hard drive, is this e-learning or CBT? There is also classroom technology such as computer projectors and smart boards, but because these are more often considered

Basic Rule 33
The important point to remember, as always, is to create a blended learning solution that is efficient and effective for your learners.

classroom media and are not used to deliver entire training programs, they don't fall under the heading of TBT per se.

The concept of TBT encompasses many different training methods. If you run across the term in your work as a trainer, consider it to be a catch-all for the delivery methods listed here.

Instructional Technology

To confuse the picture a bit more, some trainers consider themselves to be instructional technologists, that is, experts in the field of instructional technology. This term was borrowed from the field of public education where there are universities that grant degrees in instructional technology.

Most trainers who use this term are computer specialists who create various types of training programs in which a computer plays a significant role in the delivery of the program. Most of these folks are instructional designers who have specialized in computer-delivered training and want to differentiate themselves from other designers who create classroom or OJT programs.

Some instructional technologists not only create the training program, but also do the computer programming and graphics for it. Sometimes an instructional technologist is simply a computer programmer who's looking for ways to branch out. Before you bring an instructional technologist on board to help with the technological aspects of a training project, you'll want to find out exactly what it is that he or she knows and can do for you.

Experiential Learning

Experiential learning means exactly what it says. Learners gain knowledge by experiencing or doing an activity. The old apprenticeship process was almost totally experiential in nature. In the classroom, trainers practice experiential learning through games and role plays, and, of course, much of a good OJT process is experiential, as are the apprenticeships that often round out a well-designed structured mentoring program.

Computer technology has opened new possibilities for experiential learning. For example, in e-learning learners can be immersed in simulated environments and asked either to react or to change the environment itself to meet the goal of the exercise. It is also the basis for creating a job rotation aspect of a management development system, where the new or would-be managers experience the jobs of their colleagues, employees, and even their bosses.

Noted

The importance of experiential learning is that it causes the learners to think quickly, pay attention to outcomes, and learn directly from doing. They can also practice skills that would be dangerous to try in the real world, such as learning how to deal with hazmat spills. The downside is that in most cases it is difficult to control this form of learning or focus it toward desired outcomes. It also requires that the learners have a high level of self-direction.

Communications Training

Much of the non-job skill specific training done in an organization is communications training. In fact, after basic job skills training and management development it is probably the third most prevalent type of training found in companies. Depending on the organization, communications training may include programs in

- listening skills
- team building and working in teams
- presentation skills
- writing skills, such as memo and report writing
- telephone answering and message-leaving skills and procedures
- techniques for using and dealing with email and email systems
- how to hold effective meetings.

Most often, communications training is done in a classroom environment because of the need for interaction among people to practice the skills, but increasingly synchronous e-learning is being used for communications training, particularly if the organization is utilizing virtual workgroups.

Computer or Information Technology (IT) Training

This concept is basically training learners on the use of computers and computer software. There is a big need for this type of training, but almost no one does it very well.

Why is this so? One reason is that the people who design the software are more interested in the programming than in the people that need to use it. You can't blame the programmers; programs are much simpler to make work than people. But, this oversight makes the learning—and the training—hard. Another reason may be that computers and how they work are so foreign to most people that they just can't develop a good internal structure for learning how to use them or to retain that knowledge if they do acquire it.

To overcome these barriers, computer training should begin with a presentation of the basics followed by basics practice, followed in turn by a presentation of job aids for the more advanced material, and then practice on using the job aids. Unfortunately, most of the facilitators of this type of training are SMEs who find the presentation of the basics to be rather boring and quickly move along to the much more interesting nuances of the software that the learners may not ever need and certainly will not retain.

Computer training would seem to be a great candidate for SDL methods as the learner can move along at his or her own pace, learning each technique fully before moving to the next. Such training, however, has been a dismal failure, probably for two reasons. The first, as you might guess, is that software trainers are not instructional designers and, therefore, do not know how to create effective SDL programs. The second reason is that at the start of SDL, learners need a live person to help them begin the transition to becoming self-directed learners. For many learners, their first experience with self-instruction is an SDL program that teaches them how to use a piece of software. They are simply not yet ready to learn on their own.

Leadership Training

Leadership training has become another hot item in the training field in recent years. It used to be simply a topic in a company's management development training program, but somewhere along the line it declared its independence and became a separate entity.

Just about anybody, it seems, can train your company's supervisors, managers, and administrators to be better leaders. Chief executive officers (CEOs), retired athletic coaches, even former heads of state are selling videotape programs or are willing to come to your site in person (for the right price) to tell your management group how they went from rags to riches, led their teams to victory, or saved their countries from some disaster. Consultants who have spent years studying those CEOs and athletic coaches, as well as military generals, politicians, and other kinds of leaders, can provide you with programs of varying sizes and shapes that distill the wisdom of these leaders into 10 (or five or 20) principles of leadership.

It may sound like leadership training is akin to selling snake oil, and you'd be right—and wrong.

Good leadership is critically important in organizations, it always has been, and it always will be. Where these programs go wrong is their reliance on the notion that trainers can force someone else's leadership style on their own organization's leaders. To be successful, leadership training must be based on *your* organization's leadership style, not that of a famous coach or a CEO of some other company.

Your organization's leadership style comes from your own CEO. He or she is a leader and a good one, or someone else would have that position. A trainer's job in leadership training is to find out what the CEO's leadership philosophy is, and to help the rest of management support and augment it.

Customer Service Training

Customer service training has been around for about as long as there have been customers and someone to serve them. Customer service training comes in a variety of flavors, ranging from product knowledge (which is actually more sales training) to communications training to training that simply teaches people to be more understanding to how to deal with angry customers to how to manage stress.

Customer service training is very behavioral in nature. The best customer service training occurs when it is part of a system that might include customer service goals, employee recognition for great customer service, empowerment of employees to serve customers better, and assessment of customer service by both customers and outside agents to evaluate progress toward the customer service goals.

Such a system must address many training issues, but in the final analysis it is better seen as a performance intervention than simply training, with the training only one of the aspects that makes the system function.

Sales Training

Sales training usually means teaching salespeople how to sell. It is a microcosm of training in general as it include skills, knowledge (usually product knowledge) performance, and often behavioral changes. Your learners will run the gamut from the newest of newbies to seasoned professionals who have years of successful selling behind them but must now learn to do it another way.

Sales training usually is within the purview of the sales and marketing department, and that's as it should be. No other topic in the training world requires a stronger practical experience base on the part of the classroom facilitator than does sales training. And, the classroom is where most, if not all, of sales training happens. Because of its very nature, sales training seldom translates well into any SDL or TBT process. Sometimes a structured mentoring approach is useful and OJT can be a component, but the core is most often the classroom, and this is where the seasoned professionals amongst the audience can do serious damage to the credibility of any trainer who hasn't "been there and done that."

As a general trainer, you will probably want to limit your role in sales training to that of an internal consultant, helping the sales and marketing trainers to build good classroom programs, and then possibly evaluating them. Unless you have sales experience, you will probably be better off if you stay out of the classroom for sales training.

Getting It Done

This chapter has introduced you to a number of training-related concepts. Exercise 9-1 can guide your review of these concepts and help you decide which ones might merit further explanation.

Exercise 9-1. Where do you fit in?

1. Make a list of the similarities and differences between training and HPI. Considering your list, are you more a trainer or a performance technologist? Which one do you want to be? If you are not there, what is your plan for reaching that goal?

2. Plan a large-scale change for your organization by using the aspects of the formal change plan. Create a change agenda, outline your discussion plan for senior leadership, and suggest some workshops. Don't forget to state what your feedback mechanisms, reinforcements, and evaluations will be.

(continued on page 116)

Exercise 9-1. Where do you fit in (continued)?

3. Check to see if your organization uses any competency-based processes. If not, see if you can find an organization that does. How does the organization define competencies? How does it analyze for them? How does it use them? Does the usage match the definition and analysis? If not, what would you change so that the usage is valid?

4. List the various types of specialized training an organization might have. Are any of these offered in your organization? If so, are they successful? Given the charge to do so, how would you evaluate the effectiveness of each?

5. How does the concept of knowledge management relate to the creation of a learning organization? What are the characteristics of a learning organization?

So now you're a trainer. Well, maybe only in title. Now you know that there's more to being a trainer than just having the nerve to get up in front of a class and talk. This book, however, is a jumping-off point, maybe just the beginning of the beginning. You should have an idea now of what a trainer does and possibly some plan in mind for what you need to do to develop some training expertise. The other books in this series and the Additional Resources that follow this chapter can provide you with the information that you need to make that plan a reality, no matter what aspects of training you have chosen for your plan or in what order. *You can become the trainer you want to be!*

In case you're not sure of your plan, or simply need a review of everything covered in this book, exercise 9-2 is a comprehensive chart for you to use to help you map your way to training excellence.

Exercise 9-2. Your map for using this book as a guide to training.

What a Trainer Needs to Know	Why Is This Important to the Trainer?	Where Is It Covered in This Book?	Got It?
How training differs from education	To understand what a trainer is responsible for	Chapter 1	☐ Yes ☐ Almost ☐ More to Do
Instructional design	To create training programs that are effective, efficient, and reproducible	Chapters 1, 7	☐ Yes ☐ Almost ☐ More to Do
Technology-based learning, particularly e-learning	Technology is becoming the preferred method of delivery for many training programs	Chapters 1, 6, 7	☐ Yes ☐ Almost ☐ More to Do
Trainer-speak	To be able to talk like a trainer and understand what trainers are talking about	Chapters 1–9	☐ Yes ☐ Almost ☐ More to Do
Adult learning theory	To understand how adults learn so the trainer can teach them effectively	Chapter 2	☐ Yes ☐ Almost ☐ More to Do
How to analyze training needs	To find out what the training needs are of the organization the trainer is working for	Chapters 3, 4	☐ Yes ☐ Almost ☐ More to Do
How to do an audience analysis	To determine the characteristics of the people the trainer is going to train	Chapter 3	☐ Yes ☐ Almost ☐ More to Do
Analysis techniques	Allows the trainer to pick the right technique that will provide the most information	Chapter 3	☐ Yes ☐ Almost ☐ More to Do
Learning objectives	Well-written objectives provide the trainer and the learner with the blueprint for what they need to do	Chapter 4	☐ Yes ☐ Almost ☐ More to Do
How to work with subject matter experts (SMEs)	The SMEs provide the content for your training programs	Chapter 4	☐ Yes ☐ Almost ☐ More to Do

(continued on page 118)

Exercise 9-2. Your map for using this book as a guide to training (continued).

What a Trainer Needs to Know	Why Is This Important to the Trainer?	Where Is It Covered in This Book?	Got It?
How to evaluate learners and programs	Without proper evaluation the trainer does not know if learning occurred or if the program was successful	Chapters 4, 5	☐ Yes ☐ Almost ☐ More to Do
The various levels of evaluation	Understanding evaluation levels allows the trainer to choose the right type of evaluation for the evaluation data he or she needs to gather	Chapter 5	☐ Yes ☐ Almost ☐ More to Do
How to create a training plan	The training plan is the method by which the trainer keeps track of everything that needs to be done to create a successful training program	Chapters 6, 8	☐ Yes ☐ Almost ☐ More to Do
The types of training programs and how they are used	Knowing how to use various types of training programs allows the trainer to create the most effective training for any training need	Chapters 2, 3, 6	☐ Yes ☐ Almost ☐ More to Do
How to facilitate effectively	Effective facilitation skills are critical for any trainer as facilitation is what most trainers do the most of	Chapters 6, 7,	☐ Yes ☐ Almost ☐ More to Do
Using media effectively	Media such as flipcharts, handouts, and PowerPoint presentations help the learner to learn	Chapters 1, 6, 7, 8	☐ Yes ☐ Almost ☐ More to Do
What a training system is	Trainers don't create just courses, they create entire systems of training based on the various levels of needs in the organization	Chapters 1, 8	☐ Yes ☐ Almost ☐ More to Do
How to market your training	No matter how good your training is, it won't be effective unless you can convince learners to use it	Chapter 8	☐ Yes ☐ Almost ☐ More to Do

It may seem like you've covered a lot of territory in this book, but remember, you don't need to know it all at once. And, you'll have plenty of help. If there is one thing trainers like to do, it's share: They share their knowledge, share their ideas, share their stories of how they did it, so that you can do it too. Read the books, and start forming your network of trainers to talk to, and before long you'll reach the point where you look at this book and say, "Wow, I've really come a long way since I read that!"

You've started your journey already. Good Luck!

References

■ ■

ASTD. (1998a). "Basic Training for Trainers: Training Basics." *Info-line,* 8808.

ASTD. (1998b). "The Transfer of Skills Training." *Info-line,* 9804.

ASTD. (2000). "Course Design and Development." *Info-line,* 8905.

Carliner, S. (2003). *Training Design Basics.* Alexandria, VA: ASTD.

Huey B. Long and Associates. (1989). *Self-Directed Learning: Emerging Theory and Practice.* Norman, OK: University of Oklahoma Press.

Huey B. Long and Associates. (1990). *Advances in Research and Practice in Self-Directed Learning.* Norman, OK: University of Oklahoma Press.

Huey B. Long and Associates. (1992). *Self-Directed Learning: Application and Research.* Norman, OK: University of Oklahoma Press.

Knowles, M.S. (1980). *The Modern Practice of Adult Learning.* Chicago: Follett.

Kirkpatrick, D. (1994). *Evaluating Training Programs: The Four Levels,* 2d edition. San Francisco: Berrett-Koehler.

Mager, R.F. (1975). *Preparing Instructional Objectives.* Belmont, CA: Pitman Learning Inc.

Oberstein, S., and J. Alleman. (2003). *Beyond Free Coffee and Donuts: Marketing Training and Development Programs.* Alexandria, VA: ASTD.

Rosania, R. (2003). *Presentation Basics.* Alexandria, VA: ASTD.

Rosenberg, M. (2001). *E-Learning.* New York: McGraw-Hill.

Van Buren, M.E., and W. Erskine. (2002). *State of the Industry: ASTD's Annual Review of Trends in Employer-Provided Training in the United States.* Alexandria, VA: ASTD.

Additional Resources

■ ■

Because this book is dedicated to providing you with a foundation in training basics, the resource section here is a very valuable part of this book. As you might expect, ASTD (www.astd.org) is an important resource for all things pertaining to training and development. Beyond ASTD's resources, you can access thousands of books and articles that can help you become a trainer—and a great one, at that!

General Training Resources

ASTD. (1998). "Basic Training for Trainers." *Info-line,* 8808.

Rose, E. (1997). *Presenting & Training With Magic.* McGraw-Hill Trade.

Russell, S. (1998). "Training and Learning Styles." *Info-line,* 8804.

Ukens, L., editor. (2001). *What Smart Trainers Know.* Jossey-Bass/Pfeiffer.

Adult Learning Resources

Brookfield, S.D. (1991). *Understanding and Facilitating Adult Learning.* Jossey-Bass.

Knowles, M. (1980). *The Modern Practice of Adult Education: From Pedagogy to Androgogy.* Follett.

Merriam, S.B. (2001, Spring). "The New Update on Adult Learning Theory." *New Directions for Adult and Continuing Education, 89.*

Wlodkowski, R. (1998). *Enhancing Adult Motivation to Learn.* Jossey-Bass.

Zemke, R. (1995, June). Adult Learning: What Do We Know for Sure? *Training,* 31–39.

Needs Analysis

Gupta, K. (1998). *A Practical Guide to Needs Assessment.* Jossey-Bass/Pfeiffer.

Rossett, A. (1998). *First Things Fast: A Handbook of Performance Analysis.* Jossey-Bass/Pfeiffer.

Zemke, R. (1982). *Figuring Things Out: A Trainer's Guide to Needs and Task Analysis.* Perseus Publishing.

Zemke, R. (1998, March). "How to Do a Needs Assessment When You Don't Think You Have Time." *Training,* 38–44.

Training Evaluation

Kirkpatrick, D.L. (1998). *Evaluating Training Programs: The Four Levels,* 2d edition. Berrett-Koehler.

Kirkpatrick, D.L. (1998). *Another Look at Evaluating Training Programs.* ASTD.

Parry, S.B. (1997). *Evaluating the Impact of Training.* ASTD.

Phillips, J.J. (1997). *Handbook of Training Evaluation and Measurement,* 3d edition. Butterworth-Heinemann.

Phillips, J.J. (2002). *How to Measure Training Results: A Practical Guide to Tracking the Six Key Indicators.* McGraw-Hill Trade.

Phillips, J.J. (2003). *Return on Investment in Training and Performance Improvement Programs,* 2d edition. Butterworth-Heinemann.

Phillips, J.J., and R.D. Stone. (1998). "Level 4 Evaluation: Business Results." *Infoline,* 9816.

Phillips, J.J., P.F. Pulliam, and W. Wurtz. (1998). "Level 5 Evaluation: ROI." *Infoline,* 9805.

Robinson, D.G., and J.C. Robinson. (1989). *Training for Impact: How to Link Training to Business Needs and Measure the Results.* Jossey-Bass/Pfeiffer.

Westgaard, O. (1999). *Tests That Work: Designing and Delivering Fair and Practical Measurement Tools in the Workplace.* Jossey-Bass/Pfeiffer.

Classroom Training

Arch, D. (1999). *Red Hot Handouts: Taking the HO HUM out of Handouts.* Jossey-Bass/Pfeiffer.

Foshay, R., K.H. Silber, and M. Stelnicki. (2003). *Writing Training Materials That Work: How to Train Anyone to Do Anything.* Jossey-Bass/Pfeiffer.

Pike, B., and L. Solem. (2000). *50 Creative Training Openers and Energizers.* Jossey-Bass/Pfeiffer.

Rose, E. (1999). *50 Ways to Teach Your Learner.* Jossey-Bass/Pfeiffer.

Silberman, M. (1996). *Active Training: 101 Strategies to Teach Any Subject.* Pearson Allyn & Bacon.

Stoneall, L. (1997). *How to Write Training Materials.* Jossey-Bass/Pfeiffer.

Ukens, L. (2000). *Energize Your Audience: 75 Quick Activities That Get Them Started, and Keep Them Going.* Jossey-Bass/Pfeiffer.

One-to-One Training, OJT, and Job Aids

Gery, G. (1991). *Electronic Performance Support System.* Gery Associates.

Pike, B. (1999). *One-on-One Training: How to Effectively Train One Person at a Time.* Jossey-Bass/Pfeiffer.

Rossett, A., and J. Gautier-Downes. (1991). *A Handbook of Job Aids.* Jossey-Bass/Pfeiffer.

Walter, D. (2001). *Training on the Job.* ASTD.

Self-Directed Learning

Hatcher, T.G. (1997, February). "The Ins and Outs of Self-Directed Learning." *Training & Development*, 35–39.

Piskurich, G. (1993). *Self-Directed Learning: A Practical Guide to Design, Development, and Implementation.* Jossey-Bass/Pfeiffer.

Tobin, D.R. (2000). *All Learning Is Self-Directed.* ASTD.

E-Learning

Conrad, K. (2000). *Instructional Design for Web-Based Training.* Human Resources Development Press.

Cross, J., and L. Dublin. (2002). *Implementing E-Learning.* ASTD.

Horton, W. (2000). *Designing Web-Based Training: How to Teach Anyone Anything Anywhere Anytime.* John Wiley & Sons.

Horton, W., and K. Horton. (2003). *Tools and Technologies for E-Learning: A Consumer's Guide for Trainers, Teachers, Educators, and Instructional Designers.* John Wiley & Sons.

Mantyla, K. (2001). *Blending E-Learning.* ASTD.

Piskurich, G., editor. (2003). *Preparing Learners for E-Learning.* Jossey-Bass/Pfeiffer.

Piskurich, G., editor. (2003). *Getting the Most From On-Line Learning: A Learner's Guide.* Jossey-Bass/Pfeiffer.

Piskurich, G., editor. (2003). *The AMA Handbook of E-Learning.* AMACOM.

Schank, R. (2001). *Designing World Class E-Learning.* McGraw-Hill Trade.

Mentoring and Coaching

Bell, C.R. (2002). *Managers as Mentors,* 2d edition. Berrett-Koehler Publishers.

Hudson, F. (1999). *The Handbook of Coaching: A Comprehensive Guide for Managers, Executives, Consultants, and HR.* Jossey-Bass.

Kram, K.E. (1988). *Mentoring at Work: Developmental Relationships in Organizational Life.* University Press of America.

Scandura, T. (1992). "Mentorship and Career Mobility." *Journal of Organizational Behavior, 13* 169–74.

Wick, C.W. (1989). "How People Develop: An In-Depth Look." *HR Report, 6*(7): 1–3.

Instructional Design

Chapman, B.L. (1995). "Accelerating the Instructional Design Process: A Tool for Instructional Designers." *Journal of Interactive Instruction Development, 8*(2): 8–15.

Gayeski, D. (1998, April). "Out of the Box Instructional Design." *Training & Development, 52*(4): 36–40.

Hodell, C. (2000). *ISD From the Ground Up.* ASTD.

Piskurich, G.M., editor. (1999). *The ASTD Handbook of Training Design and Delivery,* 2d edition. McGraw-Hill Trade.

Piskurich, G.M. (2000). *Rapid Instructional Design: Learning ID Fast and Right.* Jossey-Bass/Pfeiffer.

Facilitation Skills

Pike, R.W. (2003). *Creative Training Techniques Handbook: Tips, Tactics, and How-to's for Delivering Effective Training.* Human Resource Development Press.

Pike, B., and A. Dave. (1997). *Dealing With Difficult Participants: 127 Practical Strategies for Minimizing Resistance and Maximizing Results in Your Presentations.* Jossey-Bass/Pfeiffer.

Pike, B., and C. Busse. (1998). *101 Games for Trainers: A Collection of the Best Activities From Creative Training Techniques Newsletter.* Human Resource Development Press.

Silberman, M. (1996). *Active Learning: 101 Strategies to Teach Any Subject.* Pearson Allyn & Bacon.

Sugar, S. (1998). *Games That Teach: Experiential Activities for Reinforcing Learning.* Jossey-Bass/Pfeiffer.

Project Management

Levine, H.A. (2002). *Practical Project Management: Tips, Tactics, and Tools.* John Wiley & Sons.

Russell, L. (2000). *Project Management for Trainers.* ASTD.

Thompson, C. (1998). "Project Management: A Guide." *Info-line,* 9004.

Training Systems and Strategies

Barbazette, J. (2001). *Successful New Employee Orientation: Assess, Plan, Conduct, and Evaluate Your Program.* Jossey-Bass/Pfeiffer.

Caffarella, R.S. (2001). *Planning Programs for Adult Learners: A Practical Guide for Educators, Trainers, and Staff Developers,* 2d edition. Jossey-Bass.

France, D.R. (1996, October). "Quick Starts for New Employees." *Training & Development,* 47–50.

Nilson, C.D. (1999). *How to Start a Training Program: Training Is a Strategic Business Tool in Any Organization.* ASTD.

Patterson, S. (2002). *The Training Managers Quick Tip Sourcebook: Surefire Tools, Tactics, and Strategies to Solve Common Training Challenges.* Jossey-Bass/Pfeiffer.

Human Performance Improvement

Brethower, D., and K. Smalley. (1998). *Performance-Based Instruction: Linking Training to Business Results.* Jossey-Bass/Pfeiffer.

Gilbert, T.F. (1996). *Human Competence: Engineering Worthy Performance.* International Society for Performance Improvement.

Hale, J. (1998). *The Performance Consultant's Fieldbook.* Jossey-Bass/Pfeiffer.

Piskurich, G., editor. (2002). *HPI Essentials: A Just-the-Facts, Bottom-Line Primer on Human Performance Improvement.* ASTD.

Robinson, D.G., and J.C. Robinson. (1996). *Performance Consulting: Moving Beyond Training.* Berrett-Koehler Publishers.

Stolovitch, H., and E.J. Keeps. (1999). *Handbook of Human Performance Technology: Improving Individual and Organizational Performance Worldwide,* 2d edition. Jossey-Bass/Pfeiffer.

Sugrue, B., and J. Fuller, editors. (1999). *Performance Interventions: Selecting, Implementing, and Evaluating the Results.* ASTD.

Thiagarajan, S. (2003). *Design Your Own Games and Activities: Thiagi's Templates for Performance Improvement.* Jossey-Bass/Pfeiffer.

Organization Development

Beitler, M.A. (2003). *Strategic Organizational Change.* Practitioner Press International.

Bolman, L.G., and T.E. Deal. (2003). *Reframing Organizations: Artistry, Choice, and Leadership,* 3d edition. Jossey-Bass.

Collins, J. (2001). *Good to Great: Why Some Companies Make the Leap . . . and Others Don't.* HarperCollins.

Rothwell, W., R. Sullivan, and G.N. McLean. (1995). *Practicing Organizational Development: A Guide for Consultants.* Jossey-Bass/Pfeiffer.

Shafritz, J.M., and J.S. Ott. (2000). *Classics of Organization Theory,* 5th edition. Wadsworth Publishing.

Change Management

Anderson, L.A., and D. Anderson. (2001). *The Change Leader's Roadmap: How to Navigate Your Organization's Transformation.* Jossey-Bass/Pfeiffer.

Argyris, C. (1993). *Knowledge for Action: A Guide for Overcoming Barriers to Organizational Change.* Jossey-Bass.

Chang, R.Y. (1994). *Mastering Change Management: A Practical Guide for Turning Obstacles Into Opportunities (Management Skills Series).* Richard Chang Associates.

Lee, W., and K.J. Krayer. (2003). *Organizing Change: An Inclusive, Systemic Approach to Maintain Productivity and Achieve Results (With CD-ROM).* Jossey-Bass/Pfeiffer.

Training Competencies

Cooper, K. (2000). *Effective Competency Modeling and Reporting With CD-ROM.* AMACOM.

Dubois, D.D. (1998). *The Competency Case Book.* Human Resource Development Press.

Parry, S. (1995). "The Quest for Competencies." *Training,* 48–56.

Spencer, L.M., and S. Spencer. (1993). *Competence at Work: Models for Superior Performance.* John Wiley & Sons.

Knowledge Management and Learning Organizations

Chawla, S., and J. Renesch, editors. (1995). *Learning Organizations: Developing Cultures for Tomorrow's Workplace.* Productivity Press.

Davenport, T., and L. Prusak. (1997). *Working Knowledge: How Organizations Manage What They Know.* Harvard Business School Press.

Marquardt, M.J. (2002). *Building the Learning Organization.* Davies-Black Publishers.

Nonaka, I., and H. Takeuchi. (1995). *The Knowledge Creating Company: How Japanese Companies Create the Dynamics of Innovation.* Oxford Press.

Rossett, A. (1999). "Knowledge Management Meets Analysis." *Training & Development, 53*(5): 62–68.

Rumizen, M. (2001). *The Complete Idiot's Guide to Knowledge Management.* Alpha Books.

Senge, P. (1994). *The Fifth Discipline: The Art and Practice of Learning.* Currency.

Wiley, D. (2002). *The Instructional Use of Learning Objects.* Agency for Instructional Technology.

Internal Consulting

Block, P. (1999). *Flawless Consulting: A Guide to Getting your Expertise Used,* 2d edition. Jossey-Bass/Pfeiffer.

Daloz, L. (1999). *Mentor: Guiding the Journey of Adult Learners.* Jossey-Bass.

LaGrossa, V., and S. Saxe. (1998). *The Consultative Approach: Partnering for Results.* Jossey-Bass/Pfeiffer.

Scott, B. (2000). *Consulting on the Inside: An Internal Consultant's Guide to Living and Working Inside Organizations.* ASTD.

Leadership Training

Blanchard, K., and S. Johnson. (1983). *The One Minute Manager.* Penguin Putnam.

Fullan, M. (2001). *Leading in a Culture of Change.* Jossey-Bass.

Kouzes, J. (2003). *The Leadership Challenge,* 3d edition. John Wiley & Sons.

Russell, L. (2003). *Leadership Training.* ASTD.

Customer Service

Carr, C. (1990). *Front-Line Customer Service: 15 Keys to Customer Satisfaction.* John Wiley & Sons.

Kamin, M. (2002). *Customer Service Training.* ASTD.

Lash, L. (1989). *The Complete Guide to Customer Service:.* John Wiley & Sons.

Leland, K., K. Bailey, G.H. Bateman. (1999). *Customer Service for Dummies,* 2d edition. John Wiley & Sons.

Zemke, R., and C.R. Bell. (1989). *Service Wisdom: Creating and Maintaining the Customer Service Edge.* Lakewoods Publications.

About the Author

■ ■

George Piskurich is an organizational learning and performance consultant based in Macon, Georgia. He provides consulting services and workshops in instructional design, management development, and performance improvement to clients throughout the country. He specializes in e-learning interventions, performance/training analysis, distance learning, design and development of self-directed and individualized learning programs for all levels of the organization, telecommuting interventions, and knowledge centers. His workshops on self-directed learning, structured mentoring, interactive distance learning, and telecommuting have been rated as outstanding by participants from many organizations.

His recent clients have included major multinational corporations for which he developed Web-enabled problem-solving and telecommuting interventions as well as a basic management program; a small technology-based organization where he designed the company's training system; a state board of education where he managed and produced an interactive satellite distance-learning intervention; and a number of telecommunications, pharmaceutical, and banking clients for whom he has created e-learning programs and other self-instructional classes on various topics.

With more than 20 years of experience in every phase of learning technology, he has been a classroom instructor in both the public and private sectors, designed development systems for managers, developed and instructed programs ranging from communications theory to computer-based training techniques, and created both industrial and health care training departments as a corporate training director.

In his specialty of self-directed learning, he has created individualized programs on topics ranging from the biological sciences to instructional and supervisory techniques, using print, slide, video, and computer-based formats.

He has written and edited many books including *Self-Directed Learning* (Jossey-Bass, 1995), *An Organizational Guide to Telecommuting* (ASTD, 1998), *The ASTD Handbook of Training Design and Delivery* (McGraw-Hill, 2000), *Rapid Instructional Design* (Jossey-Bass, 2000), *The AMA Handbook of E-Learning* (AMA, 2002), *Preparing Learners for E-Learning* (Jossey-Bass, 2003), and *Getting the Most from E-Learning* (Pfeiffer, 2003). In addition, he has written several journal articles and book chapters on various topics including customer service, structured mentoring, and corporate downsizing. He is currently writing and editing books on classroom instruction and the preparation of organizations and learners for e-learning.

He has been a presenter and workshop leader at several conferences and symposia. He is an active member of both the International Society for Performance Improvement (ISPI) and ASTD, in which he has held local and national leadership positions. In 1986 he was ASTD's Instructional Technologist of the Year and won the Best Use of Instructional Technology in Business award in 1992 for his design of distributed self-directed learning technical skills training.

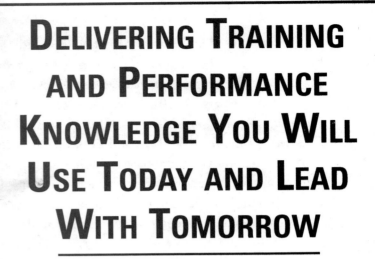